THE
REFORMATION
of
AMERICA

KARLA PERRY

MorningStar Publications

Praise for *The Reformation of America*

"Karla has important insights into some of the critical issues of our times. She has the ability to articulate them in an interesting and engaging way that is also practical."

Rick Joyner
Founder and President
MorningStar Ministries

"An enemy is not needed to destroy a great civilization. It can self-destruct by forgetting the ideas that made its language, literature, family, education, politics, economy, laws and judiciary great. Many feel the need to re-form America that no longer knows what is love, marriage, divorce, male and female, family or nation. In this powerful premier, Karla Perry explains what made America great in the first place and how it can again become a blessing to its citizens and a light to the world."

Dr. Vishal Mangalwadi
Author of *The Book That Made Your World*

"It takes an accomplished thinker and writer to capture these milestone leaders' lives and accomplishments in such a highly readable book. I do not know where you can find such an inspirational read every time you crack it open. I highly recommend the scholarship invested into it and the disciplined focus in its organization—it needs to be in every leader's library!"

Dr. Joseph Umidi
EVP Regent University
Founder, Lifeforming

"When I read the manuscript for *The Reformation of America* by Karla Perry, I was struck by the depth of research and the quality of writing. As I read this informative book, I found myself encountering points of history I did not know and received a wise and Spirit-led engagement with that history. Karla's book is an important read for any follower of Jesus Christ who desires to know their place in the current reformation that is taking place in our nation and the events that brought us to this pivotal moment in our national history."

Garris Elkins
Speaker, Mentor, and Author of *The Sound of Reformation*

"The Reformation of America, by Karla Perry, is both insightful and inspiring, and I highly recommend it. Karla demonstrates a strong grasp of history, the Founding Fathers, the U.S. Constitution, Christianity, and current affairs. She weaves these together in a provocative and powerful way to create a literary tapestry that is majestic and memorable."

Dr. Bruce Cook
Chairman, KCIA
www.kcialliance.org

"At no time in the last five hundred years has the understanding of reformation been so clearly and poignantly captured. Through exploring some of the greatest and most critical turning points of America's history, Perry brilliantly articulates centuries of complex cultural progression into its simplest form. As leaders we must know and understand the time and season we're in in order to wisely discern the critical role we can play in the formation of America's destiny. *The Reformation of America* is a deep and genuine dive into the ripe landscape on which we now stand; poised for the ultimate fulfillment of a vision now thousands of years old.

Though many have been waiting on the next great move of God, there are many who believe that God has been waiting on us. Now is the time for our courageous 'yes'. We are about to be set as a nation high upon a hill. Perry passionately invites us into this calling."

Anna Kramer
Founder, Commissioned
www.becommissoned.com

THE
REFORMATION *of* AMERICA

KARLA PERRY

The Reformation of America
by Karla Perry
Copyright ©2019
Trade Size Edition, First Printing

**Distributed by MorningStar Publications, Inc.,
a division of MorningStar Fellowship Church
375 Star Light Drive, Fort Mill, SC 29715**

**www.MorningStarMinistries.org
1-800-542-0278**

Original cover artwork by Bill Osborne.
www.BillOsborne.com. Used by permission.

Cover and Layout Design: Esther Eunjoo Jun

ISBN: 978-1-60708-700-7; 1-60708-700-6

For a free catalog of MorningStar Resources, please call 1-800-542-0278

Dedication

In loving memory of
"Grammy"
Mildred Louise Snider
(1923-2017)

Table of Contents

A Note to the Reader

America is having a worldview crisis. The ever-expanding cracks in our hull are overstressing our bulwark. We can sit and watch the water seeping into the ship. We can talk about the cracks. We can point at the severing moors. Perhaps we can name the people and institutions operating in a destructive manner thwarting our national prosperity. Maybe we can jerry-rig a few patches. However, it is unlikely that we can secure the ship without shoring up the hull from the same materials our Founding Fathers used.

When I wrote *Back to the Future: Rebuilding America's Stability*, I demonstrated that we must go backward to go forward. I cautioned that we are not trying to rebuild the past, but to stabilize the present and grow into the future that God intends for us as a nation.

In *The Reformation of America*, I provide the building material for America's stabilization. The thinkers that created America were products of a massive biblical reformation of society. The Protestant Reformation is not just church history, it is world history due to its vast scope of impact on the nations around the world. History proves that nations have been reformed to truth from a place of greater cultural decay than our own. If we become too impressed with the decay, we will have no vision for restoration.

Reformation is achieved through the work of discipling institutions, cities, and nations. In a recent social media conversation, someone asked me how nations fit into heaven. She asked if there would be an American division, a Canadian division, and so on. Her worldview could not conceive of Jesus inheriting nations, only souls going to heaven. I had never thought of nations going up into heaven, but only of heaven coming down to nations. Even using upward and downward directions is inadequate, as heaven is not a geographic place "up there." Rather, it's a spiritual realm of God's kingdom, which

1

belongs united with the physical and geographical creation. I am reminded of Jesus' prayer that God's kingdom comes on earth as it is in heaven.

Almost every chapter of this book was once an article published by *The MorningStar Journal* or The Oak Initiative under the series title *The Restoration of America*. The feedback I received on these articles were of such a nature that I knew I needed to compile them into a single book. We are living in an age of reformers. Believers are working again to bring practical reformation to cities and nations. The goal of these articles, and now this book, is to provide the history that undergirds the reforming of America.

The only thing that will right our ship is truth. Teaching the truth and living the truth in every sphere of society is the only way to restore what we are in the process of losing. I would be remiss to communicate that we have lost our foundation. If this were true, we would have decayed into full scale paganism and third world conditions on a national scale. Recognizing the truth in our land is part of the process of understanding the way forward. It did not come to us self-evidently. It is not known from common sense. It is biblical applied theology on an institutional and national scale.

Whether I am providing a profile of Noah Webster, William McGuffey, or delving into economics, education, universities, marriage, or the importance of the Bible to the development of our culture, I am providing the historical, theological, and educational material that can reform our institutions. My goal is not to simply provide a fascinating read for your enjoyment. *The Reformation of America* is a history book designed to inspire my readers to participate in the work of restoring our nation to our biblical heritage.

We each have a part to play. The Bible makes us into reformers. You have something to contribute to your nation. Now is the time to step into the active reformation of our society.

As you read this book, ask yourself this question:

"Which of these topics speaks to me the most?"

When you know the answer, send me a message through my website: www.karlaperry.com. I would love to correspond with you about the next steps in walking out the part God has given you. Maybe you are already working in one of these areas doing reformation work. If so, I would love to hear what you are doing.

Acknowledgements

No author writes alone. My gratitude to authors in the writing of this book dates to Moses, and then travels through time to Martin Luther, George Washington, Abraham Lincoln, John Locke, Noah Webster, and William McGuffey. It also includes modern and contemporary authors such as Os Guinness, Nancy Pearcey, Francis Schaeffer, and my dear friend Vishal Mangalwadi who has been an enormous support to me in the shifting of my worldview to understand the importance of the Reformation and the Bible in the creation of our modern world.

My greatest gratitude goes to my loving husband, Joseph. He is my constant support and encourager. Joseph has listened to my ideas, read, proofread, and edited my work through many revisions, and generated many creative ideas that have enhanced my work.

I am forever grateful to my mother, Patty Snider, who raised me in a Christian home and sacrificed to ensure my Christian education. She is the first who took care to give me a Christian worldview, which has been the starting point of all my writing.

Thank you also to Rick Joyner and MorningStar Publications for the publication of my articles and books.

Section I:

American Way

1

America's First President

———◆◆◆◆———

"Having now finished the work assigned me, I retire from the great theatre of Action; and bidding an Affectionate farewell to this August body under whose orders I have so long acted, I here offer my Commission, and take my leave of all the employments of public life."

(Address to Congress on Resigning Commission Dec 23, 1783)

~ George Washington

"He will become the chief of nations, and a people yet unborn will hail him as the founder of a mighty empire."[1] An old Indian Chief prophesied these words over George Washington having observed him emerge without a scratch from the Battle at the Monongahela during the French and Indian War.[2] Washington served as an aide-de-camp to General Edward Braddock. The French succeeded in killing or injuring most of the commanding officers, leaving Washington to lead the retreat and deliver a severely injured General Braddock to safety. While doing so, not one but two horses were shot out from under the young Washington, and his coat bore the holes from four musket balls. Leadership would always find George Washington.

---

1   Empires are a pagan idea. Washington would lead a nation, which is a biblical idea, not an Empire.

2   Federer, William J. *America's God and Country* (America: Fame Publishing, Inc. 1996) p. 637.

Serving in the French and Indian War prepared Washington to serve his nation, albeit yet unformed, twenty years later in the Revolutionary War as General of the American Army. Washington carried enormous personal influence as "to many persons his word was law; to all that was best in the community, everything he said had immense weight. This influence he used with care and without waste."[3] After eight long years of leading a non-professional militia army through horrific conditions, America won the war because we held on to the end without losing the war. Victory now secured, the tired and dilapidated Continental Army faced a future without their promised pension as the government formed under the Articles of Confederation had no power to force the states to compensate the men who sacrificed their lives for the freedom of the soon to be nation. Individual state governments loosely affiliated under the Articles of the Confederation did not constitute a nation. The spirit of 1776 that led to the Declaration of Independence would need the spirit of 1787 to bring about a Constitution, but this was yet unseen.

These worn out troops who deserved great honor and a good retirement for their service desired that their leader, General Washington, continue to lead them in a revolt to secure their just financial due. Washington could have refused to surrender his leadership of the Army and assumed his own well-deserved leadership of a people desperate for national leadership. Most revolutions result in the establishment of the overthrowing party becoming the new leadership with the aid of the military. But the American Revolution was not like most revolutions, and George Washington was not like most leaders of revolutions.

Washington heard of the discontent of the Army and that they were on the verge of rebellion. He appealed to their

---

3   Lodge, Henry Cabot. *George Washington. Vol II*, (Boston: Houghton, Mifflin & Co. 1898) p. 29.

honor and addressed their concerns in a prepared speech. Still, the soldiers remained unconvinced. He pulled out a letter to read to them, pausing to pull his glasses from his pocket:, "Gentlemen," he said, "you will permit me to put on my spectacles, for I have not only grown gray but almost blind in the service of my country."[4] At that moment his message conveyed directly to the hearts of his men. Successfully relinquishing his leadership, Washington retired to his beloved Mount Vernon.

Due to the unsustainable nature of the Articles of Confederation, James Madison, Alexander Hamilton, and John Jay conferred with George Washington through correspondence about gathering the state delegates to reform the Articles so that the Revolutionary War was not won for naught. The states, un-united, could not have a foreign presence. The war debts could not be collected. The Confederation of States needed to become The United States. Washington strongly supported the revision of the Articles of Confederation believing that there needed to be a federal government. However, he had no intention of leaving Mount Vernon.

The correspondence continued to arrive at Washington's home requesting his presence at the Constitutional Convention. Upon arriving, he would be asked to serve his nation once more in presiding over the Convention in Philadelphia. Preferring greatly to remain ensconced at Mount Vernon, he begrudgingly, at the age of 54, accepted the honor to serve once more. Washington believed he was nearing the end of his life as no one in his family had lived much beyond 50 years of age. He was giving up the serenity of his home to enter public service with the full weight of feeling that death was at his door.[5]

---

4   The History Place http://www.historyplace.com/speeches/washington.htm
5   Ellis, Joseph. *The Quartet: Orchestrating the Second American Revolution*, 1783-1789 (New York; Penguin Random House, LLC, 2015

Upon conclusion of the Constitutional Convention "the people of the country turned to him with universal demand that he should stand at the head of it and fill the great office of first President of the Republic."[6] Washington again responded with reluctance and then rose to the challenge to aid his country yet again.

Inside Washington's personal prayer book is penned, "Daily frame me more and more into the likeness of Thy Son, Jesus Christ." Washington also wrote in October 1789 that, "while just government protects all in their religious rights, true religion affords to government its surest support."[7] Washington walked with God and understood how the tenants of truth, derived from the Bible, gave support to this newly created nation. To use his words, "It is impossible to rightly govern the world without God and the Bible."[8]

America's President lived with the reality of the enormous responsibility of being the first President of the United States. "I walk on untrodden ground. There is scarcely any part of my conduct which may not hereafter be drawn into precedent," wrote George Washington to Catherine M. Graham on January 9, 1790. Washington continued, "under such a view of the duties inherent in my arduous office, I could not but feel a diffidence in myself on the one hand, and an anxiety for the community, that every new arrangement should be made in the best possible manner, on the other."[9] He understood that people would study his every action for generations to come as a model for the presidency. As such he knew he had to take great care in what powers he interpreted the Constitution to bestow on the President of the United States. Hence, he set Presidential

---

6   Lodge, p 41.
7   Federer p. 658 & 655.
8   Ibid p. 660.
9   Washington, George. *The Writings of Washington, Vol. X* (Boston: Hilliard, Gray & Co., 1836.) p. 69-72.

precedence being "both the nation's chief of state and its government's active chief executive." He saw the role of President as one who maintains "ceremonial leadership and administrative activism."[10] Moreover, Washington believed the President should have the authority to fire department heads as their actions reflected on the President and thus the President needed to have the power to terminate them if the situation required it. He also interpreted that the active role in administration included overseeing and instructing his subordinates, as he purportedly did frequently.[11]

Washington remained concerned about the conduct he should maintain as President, so much so that he would seek advice from Jay, Madison, and Hamilton. He would write to them concerning conduct fitting of his office, such as the propriety of him making informal visits for social or civic reasons or whether he should tour the United States during recesses of Congress to acquaint himself more with the people.[12]

Washington shaped the government toward nationalism and power over the states. When he gave the first Thanksgiving Proclamation, he requested blessings over the national government without referring also to the states, which served to irritate the states' rights advocates. Approving three new states to enter the Union, he promoted nationalism as he expanded the U.S. territory.[13] On July 8, 1789, he created the Department of Foreign Affairs by executive order. In 1789 and 1795, he issued the Thanksgiving Day Proclamation. He issued proclamations on ratification of the Creek Nation Treaty, violations of Indian treaties, and "warning citizens

---

10   Rozell, Mark J. ed. *George Washington and the Origins of the American Presidency* (Connecticut: Praeger Publishers, 2000) p. 95.
11   Ibid, p. 106.
12   Washington, George. *The Writings of Washington, Vol. X* (Boston: Hilliard, Gray & Co., 1836.) p. 456-466
13   Rozell, p. 15.

to refrain and desist" from the Whiskey Rebellion with a full pardon following those involved in the Rebellion.[14] As one can see, he had no qualms against executive orders and proclamations. He had to establish Presidential authority that had strength to last for generations to come.

In keeping with his efforts to solidify the idea of America as a singular nation, Washington upheld the Constitution even when it caused him to defer to the states. He, like his fellow Federalists, believed in a limited federal government; they did not want to create a tyranny or dictatorship, but had to establish the strength of the central government. Several times Washington denied the power of the national government and even his power as executive to defer to the states giving the reason that the Constitution warranted it.[15] Allowing the Constitution to dictate his actions, he built trust into the American people for this new government.

Washington assumed the role of Commander and Chief, which is "a President's most visible role and the one where Presidents can exhibit the greatest strength."[16] Washington even rode horseback into Pennsylvania to see that order was restored following the Whiskey Rebellion. He activated his authority as Commander in Chief by organizing the militia to provide protection from the Indians in the West. As Commander in Chief he would, at times, become a diplomat in foreign affairs holding fast to his belief in peace at all cost, even if it meant isolation. Washington, and America for that matter, had lived through enough war. Isolation became his foreign policy.

Washington had full confidence in the newly established Constitution and government, as he wrote in a letter dated

---

14 Ibid, p. 16.
15 Phelps, Glenn. George Washington and American Constitutionalism (Kansas: University Press of Kansas: 1993) p. 126-133.
16 Rozell p. 22.

January 9, 1790: "that the government, though not actually perfect, is one of the best in the world . . . I always believed, that an unequivocally free and equal representation of the people in the legislature, together with an efficient and responsible executive, was the great pillar on which the preservation of American freedom must depend."[17] He further invested his confidence in the people he represented wholeheartedly when he went on to say, "It was indeed next to a miracle, that there should have been so much unanimity in points of such importance among such a number of citizens, so widely scattered, and so different in their habits in many respects as the Americans were."[18]

That miraculous unity held together the great experiment and shaped true patriotism and citizenship. In fact, in 1790 there were no national dividing parties; there was only Republicanism. Washington indeed served in a miraculous era of national unity. He commenced his term in office by reminding the nation that, "the destiny of the Republican model of government rested in their hands."[19] Thus, Washington adhered to the most important principle of the American Republic—that America is a government of the people, by the people, and for the people.

He may very well have been able to stay on as President had he desired, for no term limits had been set. Yet, as before when he surrendered his command of the army after the Revolutionary War, he surrendered his Presidency at the end of his second term. The President proclaimed in his farewell speech that, "tis substantially true that virtue or morality is a necessary spring of popular government."[20] Thus, he strove for

17   Washington p. 69-72
18   Ibid.
19   Higginbotham, Don. George Washington Uniting a Nation (Oxford: Rowan Littlefield Publishers, Inc., 2002) p. 53.
20   Federer, p. 661

virtue and morality in his administration by constantly keeping his conduct above reproach. Of all that Washington did to shape the office of the executive, his greatest accomplishment was his conduct of integrity and superb virtue in all areas of his life. As such, upon Washington's death in December of 1799, Congressman Henry Lee eulogized, "The purity of his private character gave effulgence to his public virtues . . . Such was the man for whom our nation mourns."[21]

---

21   http://gwpapers.virginia.edu/exhibits/mourning/response.html

2

Rediscovering the American Way

————— ‹‹◆›› —————

"For America to 'work', Americans must cultivate the virtues
necessary for freedom and ensure they are passed from generation
to generation."

~ Os Guinness

When the Founding Fathers forged the Constitution,
our identity became better solidified against foreign ideas.
As time passed, the geographical divide between competing
national worldviews has all but disappeared. One need not live
in another land to adopt the culture and beliefs of that land.
Many watch in horror as American-born citizens align with
foreign terrorist groups. The marketplace of ideas has grown to
include ways of thinking that are destructive to America's future.

The Founding Fathers placed safeguards in the
Constitution against elected leaders being influenced by the
ways of foreign nations. James Madison argues the point in
Federalist Paper 62:

> The qualifications proposed for senators, as distinguished
> from those of representatives, consist in a more advanced
> age and a longer period of citizenship. A senator must
> be thirty years of age at least; as a representative must be
> twenty-five. And the former must have been a citizen
> nine years; as seven years are required for the latter. The

propriety of these distinctions is explained by the nature
of the senatorial trust, which, requiring greater extent
of information and stability of character, requires at the
same time that the senator should have reached a period
of life most likely to supply these advantages; and which,
participating immediately in transactions with foreign
nations, ought to be exercised by none who are not
thoroughly weaned from the prepossessions and habits
incident to foreign birth and education. The term of
nine years appears to be a prudent mediocrity between
a total exclusion of adopted citizens, whose merits and
talents may claim a share in the public confidence, and
an indiscriminate and hasty admission of them, which
might create a channel for foreign influence on the
national councils.[22]

Securing a nation against foreign influence is a biblical
concept. God wrote it in stone. The First Commandment is
to have no other gods besides God. The Jewish people were
forbidden to practice the ways of other nations and from
adopting their gods.

However, the Constitution protects freedom of religion
in America. We cannot outlaw the practice of any religion, for
the law that condemns one religion will condemn all religions.
At the same time, the culture of a nation is informed by
religion or the rejection of it. Removing liberty to ensure safety
is the hallmark of despotism. How do we maintain a nation
built on the Judeo-Christian worldview without undermining
the free exercise of religion?

The Constitutional safeguard of citizenry for a nine or
seven-year period no longer provides the same security against
foreign allegiances or influences. One may have never set foot
in a foreign nation and yet be fully immersed in the culture

---

22   Madison, James *Federalist Papers* #62

antithetical to the American way of life. In the 2006 DC
Comics' *Superman Returns*, Perry White asks if Superman still
stands for "truth, justice, and all that stuff" omitting the iconic
phrase, "the American way." If we do not have an American
way, we will not have an America. The thing itself will go the
way of its identity.

A nation has its own land, government, language, and way
of life. If it loses one of these it is in danger of losing the rest.
It is important to note that by the very nature that we can have
this conversation, the situation has not deteriorated to that
extent. When we can see something before it has been lost, we
have the foresight necessary to correct it and set it back on its
proper course.

The problem is that we do not know what "the
American way" is anymore. The melting pot has morphed
into something inclusive of all ways. Instead of an arena for
competing ideas, it has become a soup of equal ideas with
none being the main ingredient. How can we be "thoroughly
weaned from the prepossessions and habits incident to foreign
birth and education" if we pride ourselves on our tolerance of
all worldviews?

Our politicians come from the people and are to be
representatives of the people. If the predominate culture of
the populace is the coequal crowd absorbing all worldviews
into their identity, then how do we expect our elected
representatives to demonstrate a decidedly American way?
Another difficult question to consider is what happens if
evangelical Christianity succeeds in becoming the dominate
power structure? Would our theology cause freedom to be lost
or regained? What would our triumph look like?

The American way is no longer united with truth and
justice, but of personal belief and tolerance. This is the reality
of post-Christian America. We can look at it as a grim reality,

or as a fertile field for discipleship. There are many nations that have never been blessed to have arisen to the status of a Christian nation. America's decline can be reversed just as other nations can be discipled for the first time.

If we are on a quest to reform America to secure her future as a nation, we will need some idea of what the American way is. What is her most basic identity? What is her mission as a nation? What description can afford the way of liberty and not of legalism? Can we give it language that American citizens want to adopt that values religious, racial, and economic diversity? Can we package it into something that can be taught in the schools, colleges, and demonstrated artistically?

These are not questions for one person to answer, as they need to be owned by a larger representation of Americans. If Madison and the Founders felt it necessary to keep foreign "repossessions and habits" from the hearts of elected officials, it becomes a greater concern in our digital age.

Some nations control the internet, media, and educational curriculum to keep out unwanted information from infiltrating their national identity. These nations are not nations of liberty. How does a free nation maintain domestic identity without information control? We cannot restrict free speech or the freedom of religion in efforts to regain our identity, but we can leverage our freedom of speech and religion to this end as long as we do so responsibly.

If we, as Christians, persist in participating in the cultural war to become the dominate worldview by the manner of our might and right we could destroy the very foundation of liberty. How do we undergird that liberty without seeking to dominate people, and champion the biblical ways which provide national stability? If we live in the world without being of it, we will change the world without becoming it. If we live in the world and are of the world, we will be changed by the world. This is the tension we engage in as Christians.

The American way is unlikely to succeed as a repackaging of nostalgic Americana. It is more effective for it to be something that speaks to where we are going than only a reemergence of where we have been. It will build on the past to stabilize the future, but will form a picture of the future, rather than the past. It will be something we can grow into as a nation and will be something most Americans will want to become. If we as Christians will be a voice for our neighbors, the downtrodden, the broken, the oppressed, and the marginalized, we will have a voice worth listening to.

Our vision of the future has been limited in scope by bemoaning America's decline and eventual demise. If the church is the prophetic voice to the nations, what vision are we giving America to conform to? We will be conformed to the image we behold. What do we see? Do we want to become what we see? If not, we need a different vision.

When we prophesy to people, we do not call out their mistakes and weaknesses; we call out their strengths and promises. When we speak about our nation, we also speak from the reality of heaven rather than the reality of earth. We speak to call our nation out into her destiny rather than condemning it to its frail reality. With hope regained we can work to find our way again.

Moreover, the Scriptures speak of the bodily resurrection of all believers. Just as Jesus resurrected leaving an empty tomb, we shall resurrect with new incorruptible bodies.[23] In the same way, the world shall transform to receive an incorruptible revitalization.[24] It shall be made new. Just as a believer's old self is dead, having been crucified with Christ,

---

23 II Corinthians 5:1-5
24 Revelation 21:1

so shall the corruptible earth be "destroyed" and a new earth revealed. Revelation 21:2-5 tells us that God will come to dwell where man is and He will make everything new, the old order having passed away.

God's plan involves the revitalization of this earth. The old will pass away, but the new will come. Our assignment is to disciple nations, but there is a large part of this restoration that will only come when the King is on His throne in the New Jerusalem. Our work is akin to the bride preparing herself and her dowry (the nations) as we wait for the King to bring consummate completion; the final merging of heaven and earth.

C.S. Lewis masterfully provides a picture of nature putting on Spirit like a centaur rather than a horse and rider creating such oneness that the finest razorblade cannot pass through.[25] This oneness will be unlike pantheism where creation and God are of one substance. In contrast, this is a world made possible by the Incarnation where a mergence takes place like a mystery of marriage where the man and woman are still two and yet one.

Therefore, the Christianity that only has a vision of "going to heaven when we die" needs to push through to a larger picture of heaven coming to earth. All of creation is eagerly awaiting this merging. Furthermore, all the believers who are dwelling with the Lord are awaiting this great completion as Hebrews 11 extolls.

Hebrews gives us hope for a future that is eagerly being awaited. Both the earth and the dead in Christ are anticipating this great restoration of heaven and earth. We can join into this expectation of the new heaven and new earth where the nations receive full restoration. The work we

---

25   Lewis, C.S. *Miracles.* Chapter 16

do now is unto this picture, even though we now see dimly as in a mirror soon we shall see face to face and be transformed into His likeness.

3

How Christianity Lost American Education, Part I

———— ••◆•• ————

"A worldview that does not start with God must start with something less than God—something within creation—which then becomes the category to explain all of reality."

- Nancy Pearcey

Secularism is the malformed child of the dalliance between Protestantism and the Enlightenment. The American institutions of education delivered this heretical ward of Christianity to the populace. Essentially, Protestant control of American education ran amok and produced secularism. Understanding how this happened will help Christians to no longer see themselves as victims of secularism. It will also change the debate, allowing Christians to wrestle with the issues of influencing education in a post-Christian world.

The long-held view of evangelical Christians is that the secularists wrested control of education away from Christians by removing the Bible and prayer from our nation's schools. The truth is that Christians lost much of their influence of education in the nineteenth century, and it was fully divested by the turn of the twentieth century.

The Puritans of New England established America's first college merely six years after settling in the New World. For several decades thereafter, they had the highest per capita university-educated men. The early American colleges such as Yale and Harvard carried the New England Puritan ethic and worldview. They saw the purpose of education as a support to civilization and aimed to create virtuous citizens.[26]

In the early 1800s, most college builders were heirs to the Great Awakening, Classicism, Enlightenment moralism, and formal Christian practices. Presbyterians and Anglicans were the dominate influencers of the educational sphere. After the Second Great Awakening, Yale became the birthing place of cultural reformation, further spreading the New England Puritan heritage.[27] University historian George Marsden recounts that, "by the 1830's the combined budgets of the agencies of this 'united evangelical front' rivaled that of the federal government."[28]

The New Englanders were writing the nation's textbooks and founding colleges, towns, and hamlets. Clergyman Lyman Beecher championed the charge of preparing America as a nation to lead into the millennium.[29] Since America had no state church to civilize the nation as a whole, education became the means to this end. The Protestant/Whig ideal was to create a universal public system that encapsulated the New England worldview.[30]

However, this process was highly sectarian and other groups were beginning to protest. Catholics were excluded from this process along with any other denomination that did not share the Presbyterian or Anglican doctrine prevalent in the colleges. Attempts for state funding of alternative schools were denied, and parochial school

---

26   Marsden, George. *The Soul of the American University from Protestant Establishment to Established Nonbelief.* Oxford: Oxford University Press, 1994.

27   Ibid, p. 83

28   Ibid, p. 83.

29   Ibid, p. 84

30   Ibid, p. 87

education was generally ostracized in favor of the
leading sectarian doctrine. In order to appease a greater
constituency, the schools began to shift towards nonsectarian
teachings.

They looked for universal doctrine that could appeal
to all groups with a focus on teaching the Bible without
theology that may be particular to one group over another.
The new focus elevated morality over theology. The schools
would remain Christian and appeal to the broad base
of Christian Americans. Notwithstanding, the biblical
teachings began to drift as is evident in a comparison study
between McGuffey's first *Eclectic Readers* and the later
editions.[31]

Finally, the education molders gave way to the myth of
common sense. Morality now devoid of theology created the
assumption that moral virtues and Christian practices were
common sense and not derived only from special revelation.
Even more, science was the new fashion. Since science was
a study of God's world, it was then thought that it should
be free to lead in the discovery of truth. Science became
preeminent over, and unrestrained by, theology. The common
belief was that science would enhance the learning of truth
about God's world. Moreover, it was not conceived that it
could produce anything less than truth. Meanwhile, European
science had become unmoored from its Christian heritage,
and its conclusions drifted away from biblical truth.

Vishal Mangalwadi argues that "secularism is a Christian
heresy."[32] Reading Marsden's work, *The Soul of the American
University*, it is easy to see this truth. Secularism is Christian
morality devoid of God. It is also a deification of science. It
has become the dominant cultural molder of our modern

31   Ibid, p. 89
32   Mangalwadi, Vishal. *The Book the Made Your World*. Nashville, Thomas Nelson, 2011

world. However, it became so because Christians abdicated their role as cultural shapers to promote a more palatable universal philosophy removed from any framework of theology. The result was a culture that valued morality as a human idea and science as the way of truth.

Princeton University stood as the last bastion of Christian Presbyterian education in the mid-1800s. They held onto the infallibility of Scripture amid the Darwinian critiques of the day. The irony is that they affirmed the position of their critics by making their stand without changing the debate. Princeton President Dr. McCosh, and his protégée Warfield, appealed to science and reason to prove the reliability of the Bible. Warfield believed that if Christianity was true, as he believed it to be, science would prove it to be so. Essentially, they were looking to science to validate God's revelation, rather than to God's revelation to validate science. Instead of changing the debate and restoring the authority of God over science, they let science reign as supreme and saw it as the eventual savior of Christianity.[33]

Secularism had a quiet rise to influence because during this time, colleges transitioned from liberal arts education to a special skill education to establish authority credentials for professionals. Remanding theology to the divinity schools left a black hole of influencing philosophy on all other subjects, which secularism soon filled. Still advocating their universities to be Christian, the educators saw no necessity to apply the Bible to the sciences, history, or special skills of the industrial era. They did not see any relevance of the Bible to training engineers for the steam engine, steel industry, or electrical revolution. The age of New England Puritan influence retreated quietly into history and the modern age dawned.[34]

---

33 Marsden, p. 212-215.
34 Marsden, p. 212-215.

Moral values prevailed because they had been borrowed by secularism. The Christian character still shaped Americans to a large degree, but the theology behind that character was now only taught in church, parochial schools, and in the home.

Christians began to see America as Babylon, rather than a nation set apart to God. The mission of the church was no longer to create a great nation, but to wait for the Lord's return. For a time, the Religious Right attempted to charge back into culture and stand up against the secularization of America, but that stand failed to create a sustainable reformation.

Christians are once again realizing their mandate to disciple nations. Knowing where we went off road in the past helps us not repeat the same mistakes in the future. As Christians, it is our responsibility to lead the conversation on how to influence education without the problems of sectarianism in a nation that has grown into a culture of many religions. How do we honor the free expression of beliefs without falling into the same quagmire?

Ironically, just as Protestant education dominated the market, now secularism dominates the sphere. The Protestant-dominated education never found a way to foster inclusion without compromise, and now we are the ones excluded. Instead of creating an open marketplace of ideas, it created a stronghold of one idea that prevails to this day.

We now find ourselves, by our own doing, on the outside of cultural influence. We know we cannot force a stronghold of secular dominance to stand aside for our way of thinking. We also cannot sit on the sidelines and blame the secularists for developing philosophy in the absence of Christian influence. That would be like a parent blaming a child for its illegitimate birth. Except here we are, speaking of a philosophy rather than a created being.

Instead, we need Daniels, Josephs, and Esthers to serve in the high places of influence within the educational institutions. It is interesting to note that in reading the history of American universities, only a handful of people in each generation were the dominant players driving the philosophical shifts from the top. It does not take a mass movement of Christians to change American education; it only takes a remnant of people willing to serve in close proximity to the mind molders of education. It takes a few people, full of the Holy Spirit, who are willing to serve the nation from within the nation's schools. Now is the time for solution-oriented kingdom minded Christians to serve our nation's children through reforming the education system of America.

4

How Christianity Lost American Education, Part II

———◆◆◆◆◆———

*"A public-school system, if it means the providing of free education
for those who desire it, is a noteworthy and beneficent achievement
of modern times; but when once it becomes monopolistic it is the
most perfect instrument for tyranny which has yet been devised.
Freedom of thought in the middle ages was combated by the
Inquisition, but the modern method is far more effective."*

~ John Gresham Machen (1923)

The road to the secularization of American education
is paved with Christian controversies. Historian George
Marsden paints an accurate portrait of the failure of the
American church to establish a healthy national educational
system. This picture is buried underneath the popularized
view of the secular take-over of education. Ironically, the
unacceptable state entrenched church became transposed
upon education instead. Freedom of religion prevented an
established church, but not an established worldview of
education.

Ultimately, we created the system that now forbids our
influence. As discussed, the Puritan heritage of education gave
way to encompass a broader nonsectarian instruction. The
established leaders in education pushed to create a universal
moral character instruction that all groups would accept. The
goal was to keep this instruction universal throughout all

universities and public schools. Moreover, this gave science more room to grow without theological entanglements.[35]

The idea of the day was that science is the study of God's world. Therefore, the reasonable study of science will only yield greater discovery of truth about God's world. There was no reason to restrain something that is a truth-seeking process. Just the same, liberal Protestant Christianity became the established educational worldview. They promoted their schools as Christian and yet were extremely permissive as to the philosophy being taught so long as it was not anti-Christian, atheistic, or agnostic.[36]

A new twist in the road to secularism occurs in the 1920s and 1930s. The non-liberal Christians, which were becoming known as the fundamentalists, were awakening to their loss of presence in the established educational worldview. They saw the eroding moral character of the nation as it entered the jazz age and wanted to make a stand. The Fundamentalists blamed liberal Christians and their Darwinian evolutionary science as the harbinger of the nation's moral depravity.[37]

Leading the charge was William Jennings Bryan. He drew the line in the proverbial sand and declared that people could not believe in Darwinian evolution and the Bible.[38] They had to pick one. At this point, the liberal Christian educators were keeping agnosticism at bay as they still maintained the authority of the Bible and God's role in creation while blending in the scientific evolutionary teachings of the day. However, "the rise of the populist fundamentalism inevitably drove liberal and moderate Protestants to the defense of the freedom to teach agnosticism." Ironically, engaging in

---

35 Marsden, George. *The Soul of the American University from Protestant Establishment to Established Nonbelief.* Oxford: Oxford University Press, 1994, p. 89

36 Ibid, Chapters 5-11

37 Ibid, Chapter 17

38 I'm not arguing that Christians should embrace any form of Darwinian evolution, but that the way in which this moment in history was attended to, caused a shift in education.

the process of defending themselves opened the door to agnosticism.[39]

Instead of continuing their historical position of holding off agnosticism from the established educational view, the mind-molders of education positioned themselves to keep fundamentalism away from education. The attack mode stance of the non-liberal Christians only served to reinforce the secularization of education.[40] They failed to slow it down, and most likely expedited the process.

Marsden opines that part of the problem in this controversy was that each side refused to allow for more than one worldview to subsist in education. Nowhere in the history of American education do we find a viable idea being proposed for permitting a laissez-faire environment where multiple views could compete for influence. Secular humanism is the established view today because no model was ever created for more than one worldview in education.[41]

There is no such thing as a neutral worldview that all can ascribe to without losing freedom to think. Presently, Christians want to be the established worldview once again. The secularists are blamed for keeping Christianity out of the educational system, and yet Christian control of education is the largest contributor to American secularization.

Perhaps Christians who are interested in the education mountain can study its history and propose an innovative plan to de-establish the one worldview system of public education. This will allow competing views of influence, but it will remove the idea that one group ought to force everyone else to think their way. The freedom to believe, think, and worship as one desires is at the bedrock of American heritage. Removing this freedom and trying to create a forced way of

---

39   Ibid, p. 328
40   Ibid, Chapter 17
41   Ibid, p. 329

thinking has failed miserably. Let the Bible rise to the top because we succeeded in persuading educators of its truth rather than because a law forces it to be taught.

Restoring education would then seem to be a matter of restoring freedom to education which will include the freedom of Christian influence. American education needs leaders at the helm that can create a new system which promotes true freedom of religion rather than the establishment of religion or non-religion. Remember, where the Spirit of the Lord is there is liberty.

5

The Evangelical Movement

———◆◆◆◆◆———

"Do all the good you can,
By all the means you can,
In all the ways you can,
In all the places you can,
At all the times you can,
To all the people you can,
As long as ever you can."

~ John Wesley

Evangelical is a term rightly applied to a large spectrum of Christians. Some Christians embrace this identity, some are ignorant of it, and others want to distance themselves from it. No matter our category of preference, we are all, most likely, in the dark about its history. Knowing this history can reconnect our present to our past heritage and shore up the foundation of something that has become more defined by modernity than by its history.

Evangelical Christians have deep roots dating back to the middle of the eighteenth century. The first evangelicals were Anglican church members who had a conversion experience that resulted in them becoming serious about living out their Christian faith. As a result, they changed the way they lived to conform to a new serious life devoted to applying the Bible to their lives and serving their communities.

Instead of sending their children to boarding schools, as was the custom of the day, they educated them at home. Households, which included the family and servants, met together for pray and devotions daily. Sundays were dedicated as a day of rest to such an extent that children had Sunday games and toys designed to teach them the Bible. Evangelical gentlemen kept strict accounting of their days, noting the hours spent in prayer, Bible reading, and constructive work. Women gave themselves to raising their children, tending their families, and taking up the cause of the poor.[42]

If we are getting the idea that this was a glorious time of Christian living and fruitfulness, we would only be looking at the wheat without the tares. The serious devotion of the Evangelicals included a strong legalistic lifestyle and expectations. We see this illustrated in the Victorian literature of the day, such as the orphanages depicted in Charlotte Bronte's *Jane Eyre* or Charles Dicken's *Oliver Twist*. We can find a lot to reproduce from the hardworking Christians of this era and a good deal we do not want to perpetuate.

A reformative movement often carries with it an extreme element that begins to fade once the reformation has taken hold. Such movements are prone to over-emphasis and over-correction. However, history proves that despite some of the extremes, there was real fruit that came out of the Evangelical movement that swept through Victorian England. I am confining this history to the Anglican church Evangelicals, but John Wesley, one of the early leaders of this movement, birthed the Methodist church that took this movement to the poor as their primary focus.

---

42   Bradley, Ian. *The Call to Seriousness: The Evangelical Impact on the Victorians*, Lion Books; London, November 17, 2006.

Successful enterprises followed the ventures of the first Evangelicals. Continuing into the nineteenth century, we find the emergence of William Wilberforce and the Clapham Sect. Wilberforce, as we know, ended the slave trade by his persistent work as a long-standing member of Parliament. His successor, Anthony Ashley Cooper, the Seventh Earl of Shaftesbury, took up the cause of the poor working conditions of the nation's factory workers.

The Evangelicals were a separatist group. They were not welcome in the Church of England. Their call to seriousness and dedication to seeing personal conversions were not shared by the established church of the time. Instead of starting their own church community, these Anglican Evangelicals installed their own people into the priesthood through the proper channels of becoming a priest. Consequently, local parishes with evangelical priests at the helm welcomed and promoted the evangelical way. This was the *modus operandi* of the Evangelicals.

When the East India Trading Company forbid Evangelicals from sending missionaries to India because they were concerned the missionary work would interfere with their profits, the Evangelicals simply became the board members of the company and changed the procedure in their favor. Notable Evangelical, Dr. Charles Grant, also worked from inside the company aiding the work of William Carey and William Wilberforce.

Branching into education, Evangelicals targeted royals and aristocrats by becoming their children's nursemaids and tutors, teaching the aristocrats' children in the ways of the Lord. Moreover, schools were developed for the poor. Sundays were the only days the poor children had free to learn since they worked in the factories six days a week. Robert Raikes began the Sunday School Movement, which consisted of five and half hours of schooling each Sunday. We now only know of Sunday school as the traditional hour of Bible instruction preceding a Sunday service.

Evangelicals also formed a Religious Tract Society that distributed 500 million copies of 5,000 separate tracts, printing approximately 20 million per year. Using creative ingenuity, the Evangelicals paid the people who distributed the city's obscene material more than their normal day's wages to distribute the tracts instead. These tracts were not the simple short Roman Road tracts we know today. These were well developed teachings on a variety of topics, including the necessity of church attendance, giving to missions, and the call to seriousness.

Victorian era politicians were a sorry lot. Corruption reigned unchecked. The politicians alienated the middle class and the political system itself became a weak institution. The Evangelicals jumped into the fray. Becoming great statesmen, they raised the bar for the whole system of politicians.[43] History shows us that it did not matter how corrupt the times were. Men and women who were serious about their God-given mission to serve their nation changed the status quo through hard work and determination.

Today we see the power of organizations. Businesses like Walmart, Target, and Starbucks have immense social and political power to change culture. When the South Carolina Confederate Flag debate raged across the nation, Walmart, Sears, Amazon, and other distributors removed the flag from their shelves, thereby participating in the shaping of culture. According to *Newsweek*, corporate America's support of gay marriage undergirded the movement's success.[44] According to

---

43 Ibid.
44 Cadei, Emily, *Newsweek: How Corporate America Propelled Same-Sex Marriage.* June 30, 2015. http://www.newsweek.com/2015/07/10/shift-corporate-america-social-issues-become-good-business-348458.html

Fortune Magazine,

> In many ways, Walmart is the corporate face
> of America. With this position as the world's
> biggest retailer comes the power to influence
> other corporate actors, setting business
> trends and consumer standards, and possibly
> shaping cultural norms.[45]

Corporate America is a huge field ripe for influencing the nation. Christians can be on the boards of these corporations just the same as anyone else. Instead of bemoaning the success of these corporate giants, we should be excited at this new avenue of successful cultural molding. How many local businessmen and women are involved in our city's politics? Are we getting to know these people in our cities? Are we serving them without an agenda to get something from them?

Evangelicals shout, protest, complain, and sometimes boycott, but we are not thinking the way our predecessors did. We want the secular world to stop shaping culture according to their worldview. This is not going to happen. We have the same tools available to us to shape culture; we have just abdicated them to the world. Our job is not to stop the world from shaping culture; it is to start being the shapers of culture. God gave man dominion over the earth. Non-Christians are not doing anything wrong by having dominion over the spheres in which they have influence. They are doing the job given to man; they are just doing it under a different master. We would have more success influencing the dominion people have instead of trying to make them stop being so good at changing the culture.

---

45 Weathersby, Danielle & Day, Terri, *Fortune: How Walmart Could Get Congress to Reform America's Gun Control Laws*. June 25, 2015 http://fortune.com/2015/06/25/how-walmart-could-get-congress-to-reform-americas-gun-control-laws/

Typically, instead of changing culture, we create subculture. We create subpar sanctified imitations of the world's culture so that we can enjoy music, art, entertainment, education, and media without being in the world. Our forefathers stepped into the fray. They went into the world. The Evangelicals were in Parliament, on the board of the East India Trading Company, on the mission field, establishing schools for the poor, and tutoring the children of the wealthy. In every conceivable way they could serve society and be the influencers and molders of the atmosphere of their cities, they were hard at work.

Modern Evangelicals like to be the victims of the secular influencers. We fight from a place of defeat. We are the marginalized group. We believe we cannot be salt and light in the public schools, in Congress, in mainstream media, etc., because the secular forces will not let us. We errantly see our mission as stopping their work instead of doing or influencing the work ourselves. No one let Wilberforce end the slave trade. No one stepped aside so that the Evangelicals could do mission work in India. No one bent to the will of a well-orchestrated protest. No one needed to even know the end game of these dedicated workers. They were present in the world but living a life distinct from it. We know of them today because of their success. We are products of their legacy. Will we join with our evangelical history and leave a legacy of occupation or will we continue to be protesters on the sidelines of history?

6

A History Lesson

"The Bible is for the Government of the People, by the People, and for the People."

~ John Wycliffe (1384)

American history fails us in one respect—it is confined to America. The history begins with a Christianized people with no understanding of how that came to be. Like the Founders, we have come to believe the Christian worldview is self-evident. In so doing, we deem it a product of an enlightened or educated people. However, we have not studied our history back far enough to find that the American system is not the development of modern man, but that modern man is a development of the Bible's impact on a nation.

Thus, American history ought not to begin with the foundation of America, but with the foundation of a Christian nation, as it rose out of the ashes of fallen Rome. Our Western story begins as an ascent out of paganism when Christians shaped the culture of Medieval Europe.[46] From there the culture of a discipled Great Britain expanded through colonizing India, Africa, and the Americas. As the East India Trading Company began its trade exploitation of India, William Carey commenced his mission work to enable India to become independent of Britain as its own great nation. The

---

46   Stark, Rodney. *The Rise of Christianity* San Francisco, Harper, 1997

British government was uncertain as to whether it wanted to invest in India in this manner, but William Wilberforce and Charles Grant worked tenaciously to establish political support for discipling India.

Charles Grant, an elite member of the East India Trading Company, planted evangelical Christians in key positions to serve the Lord's interest in India and to help curb the economic exploitation of India's resources. What is interesting is that Europe forgot its former pagan life. Carey wrote letters to remind Parliament that India was no different than Europe once was. He explained that Christianity was not the proud result of an educated people, but that an educated people were a result of the teachings of the Gospel. He reminded them of their humble origins.[47]

Paul did the same thing in the New Testament. He would write to a church and remind them of what life was like before they were followers of Christ. Likewise, we would do well to heed the same reminder. In America, we have the blessed heritage of a nation that began from Christian origins. Yet, we cannot forget that is only because the work of Christianizing the culture had already begun centuries before in Europe. The Christianization of culture survived many failures and has experienced many successes. The history is not glorious, it has periods of great corruption, and yet the church survived again and again.

America's history is so very young compared to the history of England. Decadence and depravity have entered our story many times, and yet the church in America continues. Great Awakenings have revived the Christian culture several times, and we are approaching another even greater one.

There is no doubt that America has been pulling away from her heritage, and there are many reasons this has come to pass. But to see her future without hope is to not see at

47   Mangalwadi, Ruth & Vishal. *The Legacy of William Carey: The Model for the Transformation of a Culture*, United States, Crossway Books, 1999

all. Church history is far more expansive than our short American history. The results of a discipled nation remain strongly present in America, only we do not know it because we do not know history.

Americans take for granted that sense is common, for we have not experienced a land where it is not. It was not common in Rome, and it is not common in the many undiscipled nations of the world. It is not common here in America. Sense is not something that civilized men have in common. It is something that civilizes men because it comes from being discipled in the ways of the Lord. The farther one is from that discipleship, the more one lacks sense.

If we do not understand that common sense is a myth, we become surprised by the way unbelievers live. We are appalled by their sin as if they are acting unnatural. We think they deliberately choose not to follow the ways of God and blame them for not sustaining a healthy society. Unbelievers are prone to sin. They are prone to foolish living. Secularists discipled America because the church stopped discipling our nation.

To quote Vishal Mangalwadi, "Secularism is a Christian heresy."[48] It is the structure of the Christian worldview devoid of its supernatural implications. It is Christian principles without God. Therefore, modern atheists write books judging God, because they borrow from Christian morality to hold God accountable for where they believe He has failed to live up to the universal standard of good. However, there is no universally agreed standard; there is only the revealed standard of God Himself and the teachings about how to live life recorded in the Bible. Atheists do not know their history either. If they did, they would know that the most famous atheist, Nietzsche, wrote that the death of God also means the death of Christian morality. You cannot have one without the other. Christian righteous living is inextricably tied to the Christian God.

---

48   Mangalwadi, Vishal. *The Book the Made Your World*. Nashville, Thomas Nelson, 2011

Secularism is not a group of people who came to America to subvert Christianity. It is a people with the remnants of a Christian worldview stripped of its foundation and left in the wind to develop American culture without the aid of true Christians. It is like dead tree branches no longer attached to the living tree and root system. It is not sustainable, for its life source abandoned it. The church cut off the branches that discipled the "secular" areas of culture and left culture to be discipled by the dead branches. The world did not do this to us, we did it to them. We are doing it still.

When secularism gives way, it gives way to paganism. Sense is not sustained without continued discipleship. Secular culture cannot, by itself, wake up and reconnect to the church. Entropy takes effect, which results in paganism. With paganism, you have a return to the base sinful nature of un-discipled man. You also have spirituality of nature worship and the like. It is out of that ground that Christianity first began to shape the national identity of the Western world. Thus, even if this were to happen, all is not lost.

The American culture is toying with paganism and animism. We see this in movies like James Cameron's *Avatar*. The environmental movement tries to find its home in spiritualizing nature, which is one reason many Christians avoid the movement. But such a philosophy will only end the movement, for it will make nature something that is dominate over us, instead of something we have dominion over. Only in Christianity can man have dominion over nature and be its caretaker.[49] Worshiping cows leads to a malnourished over population of cows. Stewarding cows will keep them healthy and in optimum condition for proper usage.

The more we trace the roots of the American culture, the more we will find their true home in the Bible. Sustaining

---

49   Mangalwadi, Vishal BLUE: *Mother Earth Should Take Care of Us.* Video by Vishal Mangalwadi. https://www.youtube.com/watch?v=8XeO0MQqimc

American heritage is a job of believers to disciple those in proximity to their influence. It is entering all the areas of culture that the church left to the world to disciple and being the salt and light we are called to be. We will not make much progress trying to get the world to stop being the world. However, we are the light of the world because Jesus lives in us, and darkness cannot overcome the light.

Any prognosis that allows for darkness to overpower the light is a false prognosis. The only way such a thing can happen is if we extinguish, or hide, our light. We are unable to be the victims of any system of secular or pagan expansion. The church is alive in America and is waking up to her responsibility to disciple our nation. With the foundation laid for effective reformation, coupled with another Great Awakening emerging, I do not see how we could have anything but great hope for our nation.

7

Why the Founders Chose a Republic

———◆◆◆◆———

"The American 'unum' has been lost since the Sixties. If this
continues, there will soon be no unifying American identity and
vision to balance the 'pluribus,' and the days of the Republic will
be numbered."

~ Os Guinness

When Benjamin Franklin emerged from the
Constitutional Convention that convened from May 25
to September 17, 1787 to address the problems facing the
post-Revolutionary War America, he was asked by a passerby
what was the outcome of the assembly. Franklin responded,
"it's a Republic, if you can keep it."

The great American government created by those
men in 1787 was not anything akin to the current or past
governments of the world. It was not just a democracy; it
was a Republic. Therein lies an important distinction.

The best source on the meaning of the Constitution and
the authority on the government created by the Founders
is a collection of essays written in 1787 to the average
American, posted in the newspapers of the day. These essays
were written under the pseudonym of Publius by Alexander
Hamilton, James Madison, and John Jay.

A group, known as anti-Federalist, opposed the creation of a centralized government. They gave speeches and wrote articles arguing against the states ratifying the proposed Constitution. The fate of the nation hung in the balance. The Federalists, eager to support the newly proposed Constitution, began to publish their own essays in its defense. Therefore, the Federalist essays were an apologetic, a defense, for this Constitutional Republic form of government. Today we know these documents as *The Federalist Papers*.

The authors explained that they were not designing America to mirror the democracy of the Greeks. They had great concern that such a government would be detrimental to America. Moreover, Publius briefly discussed the various nations using the term "republic" or "democracy" with ill regard to the actual meaning of the terms. They illustrate that no government exists that accurately exemplifies what they have in mind to create for America. While the Greeks were a pattern of democracy and England a form of a representative government, neither nation truly modeled a real republic. In other words, what the Founders were proposing had not been done. They borrowed the word "republic," but not the political philosophy of what constitutes a republic.

James Madison, in Federalist Essay 14, provides the simple distinction between a democracy and a republic. He writes, "in a democracy, the people meet and exercise the government in person; in a republic they assemble and administer it by their representatives and agents."[50]

He proceeds to enumerate the benefits of a republic over that of a democracy. He writes that "A democracy

---

50   Madison, James. The Federalist Papers, Penguin Books: New York, #14

consequently will be confined to a small spot. A republic may be extended over a large region."[51]

Thus, one of the predominate reasons for a republic is that it can effectively govern a larger number of people whereas a democracy is limited in reach to the number of people who can travel to an assembly and be a small enough group that the equality does not triumph over practicality of governance. Just think if five hundred people in a neighborhood want to democratically decide on a matter. Nothing would ever be accomplished. The population able to be governed directly by an assembly of all the people would have to be incredibly small, and thus this method would be ineffective to govern a nation.

The people would also need to be competent enough to participate at such an involved level. This would require specialized knowledge for every American with direct adverse effect upon the whole if people did not participate. With the lack of participation in today's politics of the whole in simply electing representatives, we can see how detrimental a democracy would have been over that of a republic.

Moreover, the Federalists argued that in such a democracy mob rule or factions could and would arise and prevent the voice of the minority from being heard. The desires of the mob could overrule the issuance of justice and trample on the rights of those who do not have as much influence or numbers.

Consider the words of James Madison in Federalist Essay 10:

> From this view of the subject it may be concluded that a pure democracy, by which I mean a society consisting of a small number of citizens, who assemble and administer the government in person, can admit

---

51   Ibid

of no cure for the mischiefs of faction. A common passion or interest will, in almost every case, be felt by a majority of the whole; a communication and concert result from the form of government itself; and there is nothing to check the inducements to sacrifice the weaker party or an obnoxious individual. Hence it is that such democracies have ever been spectacles of turbulence and contention; have ever been found incompatible with personal security or the rights of property; and have in general been as short in their lives as they have been violent in their deaths. Theoretic politicians, who have patronized this species of government, have erroneously supposed that by reducing mankind to a perfect equality in their political rights, they would, at the same time, be perfectly equalized and assimilated in their possessions, their opinions, and their passions.

A republic, by which I mean a government in which the scheme of representation takes place, opens a different prospect, and promises the cure for which we are seeking.[52]

The Federalists were keenly aware of the turbulence that a democracy would cause if all people in a nation were assembled to decide matters for themselves. Instead, they advocated that we select representatives from amongst ourselves that we trust and know to be wise to see to these matters on our behalf. They suggested that the terms that these representatives have in office remain limited to a certain number of years to protect us from their gaining too much power as well as allowing us to replace the ones who failed to adequately perform their duties in a manner that truly represented the best interest of the people. They believed

---

52   Ibid, #10

that to have these people devoted to this process, serving the citizens of this nation, would establish a more capable system of government for the benefit of the people.

Madison eloquently highlights the role of the people in selecting representatives and the duty those representatives have to the people who selected them. In a republic, the views of the people are refined and given a voice "by passing them through the medium of a chosen body of citizens, whose wisdom may best discern the true interest of their country, and whose patriotism and love of justice will be least likely to sacrifice it to temporary or partial considerations."

Madison argues that "Under such a regulation, it may well happen that the public voice, pronounced by the representatives of the people, will be more consonant to the public good than if pronounced by the people themselves, convened for the purpose." He further suggests that "men of factious tempers, of local prejudices, or of sinister design, may by intrigue, by corruption, or by other means, first obtain the suffrages [votes], and then betray the interests, of the people." If this happens, Madison defends that the republic is "favorable to the election of proper guardians of the public weal." Therefore, the system is set up in such a way that the public can remove representatives when their term expires. Moreover, checks and balances are in place to limit the damage that can be done during such a term of betrayal.[53]

The Federalists supported and defended the idea that the powers of the general government were limited. The state governments were to care for the matters in their respective reach that were outside of federal jurisdiction. This idea is enumerated in the 10th Amendment of the Bill of Rights. Madison argued that if the federal government were ever

---

53   Ibid

to abolish the governments of the states, they "would be compelled by principal of self-preservation, to reinstate them in their proper jurisdiction."[54]

Therefore, this nation is truly made up of one central republic and fifty mini-republics in the forms of the fifty state governments which are also representative democracies. In so doing, it is important to note that America is a democracy, but not in the extreme where each person participates directly in the governmental process, but where each of us are collectively represented. A republic is a form of democracy altered to provide the application to a large number of people with a variety of cultures that have valuable contributions to the whole.

With the power of selecting representatives in the hands of the people, citizens "will be more likely to centre in men who possess the most attractive merit and the most diffusive and established characters".[55] Thus, when Benjamin Franklin, by his famous statement, charged the American people with the duty of keeping the Republic, he invoked the responsibility of the people to be actively involved in selecting worthy representatives and paying attention to their actions while in office.

If the people fail to be active patriotic citizens, there is no voice for the elected representatives to represent. They will become people who serve their own interests and the American government will not be sustainable. It is our duty as citizens to keep the Republic and not shirk our responsibility off on others to vote and care about the political process. The process affects everyone, and it is the duty of every citizen to be knowledgeable and active members of this Republic.

---

54   Ibid, #14
55   Ibid, #10

Franklin's statement "it's a Republic, if you can keep it" rings true for our generation as much as for the Founders' generation. The challenge that remains to pervade the present and forthcoming generations is, "Will you keep it?"

Section II:

Making America

8

John Locke, Part I

-----◆◆◆◆------

"The Bible is one of the greatest blessings bestowed by God on the children of men. It has God for its author; salvation for its end, and truth without any mixture for its matter. It is all pure."

- John Locke

Jefferson penned the Declaration of Independence, but it was Locke who provided the political philosophy it popularized. Modernity champions John Locke as a secular Enlightenment fellow, at best a Deist.[56] In actuality, he espoused a Christian worldview, deriving his political philosophy from the Bible.

The Christian origins of American political philosophy provide the values that sustain the entire system. A structure that has lost its supporting foundation is but an empty shell. For a time, the infrastructure will hold if the values remain in the culture, but once they have faded it cannot continue to stand. American values have become so far removed from their biblical mooring that they can no longer continue unsupported. G.K. Chesterton opines that every revolution is a restoration.[57] If we illuminate the true history of America and make it available to the common citizens, we can begin to see such a restoration.

---

56   A deist is one who believes God set creation into motion and is no longer involved in the affairs of men.

57   Chesterton, G.K. *What's Wrong with the World.* Dover: New York, 1910 & 2007 p. 22

John Locke (1632-1704) was an instrumental influencer of the Founding Fathers. As such, it is crucial to understand the true origin of Locke's philosophy. Gary T. Amos, former professor at Regent University School of Law, writes that, "Carl Becker, more than anyone else, is the Aesop behind the 'deistic American' fable.[58]" Becker wrote a book *The Declaration of Independence: A Study on the History of Political Ideas* in 1922 that was republished in 1942 on the deistic foundations of the Declaration of Independence wherein he purported Locke to be a Deist. Just the same, Becker is not the first to link Locke to Deism.

According to Dr. Harald Hoffding [1843-1931], professor at the University of Copenhagen, Locke was accused of deism in his own lifetime. As a result, Oxford University chose not to recognize Locke's works. This conflict occurred after Locke, having visited a Quaker assembly, began to profess the freedom of women to proclaim/preach God's love.[59] This was not well received by theologians and sparked controversy. Just the same, Hoffding writes, Locke "considered himself a believing Christian . . . and read the Bible diligently."[60] Locke, however, was not orthodox in his doctrine and preferred to align himself with less dogmatic circles of Christianity. As a champion of freedom, his political philosophy applied biblical truth to social government. It was as much of an intellectual experiment as the practical execution of it was in the founding of America. Never had these ideas been encapsulated into the foundation of a nation and implemented. The American Experiment brought Locke's works to life.

The Declaration of Independence embodied Locke's *Second Treatise of Government*. Richard Henry Lee, a signer of the Declaration, stated that the Declaration was "copied

---

58 Amos, Gary T. *Defending the Declaration* Wolgemuth & Hyatt: Brentwood, 1989, p. 51-55.
59 Hoffding, Herald. A History of Modern Philosophy: A Sketch of the History of Philosophy. Andover: Cambridge, 1900 p. 381.
60 Ibid, p. 381.

from Locke's Treatise on Government."[61] Locke directly refers to Scripture one hundred and fifty-seven times in the Second Treatise, and over a thousand times in his First Treatise of Government.[62] Moreover, he frequently cites theologian Richard Hooker in his political works.[63]

Joseph Carring, Ph.D., who specializes in American political theory and government, wrote the introduction to the Barnes and Noble Library edition. Within his introduction he writes emphatically, "The Second Treatise should be read by the citizens of any liberal democracy as a reminder of the principles upon which their government is based, and the reason for which they believe it preferable to any other."[64]

Jefferson utilizes the Lockean language "Laws of Nature and Nature's God" in the Declaration's first paragraph. This is not deistic terminology. To quote from the Second Treatise:

> [T]he law of Nature stands as an eternal rule to all men, legislators as well as others. The rules that they make for other men's actions must. . . be comfortable to the Law of Nature, i.e., to the will of God, of which that is a declaration, and the fundamental law of Nature being the preservation of mankind, no human sanction can be good or valid against it.[65]

Moreover, he quotes Richard Hooker agreeing that the "laws human must be made according to the general laws of Nature, and without contradiction to any positive law of Scripture, otherwise they are ill made."[66] Locke considered the Law of Nature as the will of God.

---

61 Barton, David "John Locke: Deist or Theologian" http://www.wallbuilders.com/libissuesarticles.asp?id=106

62 Ibid.

63 Ibid.

64 Locke, John. Second Treatise of Government. Barnes and Noble: New York, 1690 and 2004, p. xv

65 Ibid, p. 74

66 Ibid, p. 141

Locke believed that men are "the workmanship of one omnipotent and infinitely wise Maker."[67] He continues that we are all "the servants of one Master, sent into the world by His order and about His business; they are His property, whose workmanship they are made to last during His, not one another's pleasure."[68] Governing authorities were then also subject "to the laws of God and Nature. Nobody, no power can exempt them from the obligations of the eternal law."[69] This is because "where there is no judicature on earth to decide the controversies amongst men, God in heaven is the judge. He alone it is true, is judge of the right."[70] Deism teaches God created the world and left it to its own ways. Locke speaks of God who is present in the affairs of men.

It is impossible to even peruse Locke's works without coming away with an understanding that Locke pulls heavily from the Bible in forming his political philosophy. In so doing, it is important to read his Second Treatise to understand why the American system, as it originated with the Founding Fathers, need not be reorganized, but restored.

---

67   Ibid, p. 4
68   Ibid, p. 4
69   Ibid, p. 108
70   Ibid, p. 136

9

John Locke, Part II

<hr />

"The end of law is not to abolish or restrain, but to preserve and enlarge freedom."

~ John Locke

C.S. Lewis astutely recommended that a person ought to read one book of antiquity to every two books published in the present era. Due to the present state of the Union, it would seem we could merit from study of the literary works that shaped our political history. One such treasure of antiquity is John Locke's *Second Treatise of Government*. Wherein, Locke adeptly addresses the issues facing our times by providing a biblical philosophical framework that underpins our founding documents.

One essential theme throughout this work is that government can only be given the authority that people can freely give. Locke writes:

> Though the legislative, whether placed in one or more, whether it be always in being or only by intervals, though it be the supreme power in every commonwealth, yet, first, it is not, nor can possibly be, absolutely arbitrary over the lives and fortunes of the people. For it being but the joint power of every member of the society given up to that person or assembly which is legislator, it can be no more than

those persons had in a state of nature before they entered into society, and gave it up to the community. For nobody has absolute arbitrary power over himself, or over any other, to destroy his own life, or take away the life or property of another.[71]

His premise is that we cannot grant a person or group of people power over ourselves that we have no authority to dispense with. Our responsibility to live within the framework of biblical morality cannot be given away to a governmental power without usurping our God-given freedom. We have not the power to give away what God has given to us at the ultimate cost. If our freedom was that important to Him, it ought to be protected. Locke states, "for God having given man an understanding to direct his actions, has allowed him a freedom of will and liberty of acting."[72]

In so doing, we cannot agree to give away the rights of another. Locke explains, "The supreme power [government] cannot take from any man any part of his property without his own consent. For I have truly no property in that which another can by right take from me when he pleases against my consent. Hence it is a mistake to think that the supreme or legislative power of any commonwealth can do what it will, and dispose of the estates of the subject arbitrarily, or take any part of them at pleasure."[73] For example, since I cannot enter my neighbor's home and take what I desire for my own needs, neither can I agree to legislation that can plunder the goods of another for the sake of the whole. This concept borrows from the scriptural precept to do unto others as you would have them do unto you. This one biblical value applied to a national level would alleviate most unjust legislation.

Some feel that the way to help those in need is to have government programs that gather taxes from some to allocate goods and services to others. However, it does not change

---

71   Locke, John. *Second Treatise of Government.* Barnes and Noble: New York, 1690 and 2004, p. 74
72   Ibid, p. 30.
73   Ibid, p. 76

the fact that they cannot make that choice for others. It is a morally illegal vote to give away the property of another for the purpose of granting it to one or more deemed in greater need of it. This is Locke's message.

In so doing, Locke directly addresses the pressing issue of our day; government healthcare. He writes clearly on this point in *A Letter Concerning Toleration*:

> The care, therefore, of every man's soul belongs unto himself, and is to be left unto himself. But what if he neglect the care of his soul? I answer: What if he neglect the care of his health or of his estate, which things are nearlier related to the government of the magistrate than the other? Will the magistrate provide by an express law that such a one shall not become poor or sick? Laws provide, as much as is possible, that the goods and health of subjects be not injured by the fraud and violence of others; they do not guard them from the negligence or ill-husbandry of the possessors themselves. No man can be forced to be rich or healthful whether he will or no. [74]

The American people have, by and large, lost sight that people are responsible for their own choices. Freedom is restricted from the whole when the errant choices of some compel the few to control the many. Misplaced compassion causes the consequences of irresponsibility to be thwarted. Restricting freedom aggravates the problem instead of correcting it.

Locke emphasizes that "the end of the law is not to abolish or restrain, but to preserve and enlarge freedom."[75] In so doing, "the law," he explains, "in its true notion is not so much the limitation as the direction of a free and intelligent agent to his proper interest, and prescribes no farther than

---

74   Locke, John. A Letter Concerning Toleration. 1689. http://presspubs.uchicago.edu/founders/documents/amendI_religions10.html

75   Locke, John. Second Treatise of Government. Barnes and Nobel: New York, 1690 and 2004, p. 30

is for the general good of those under the law."[76] America has forgotten that the Founders established a constitutional government to enable, not prohibit, freedom.

Despite the often-venerated status of our illustrious Founding Fathers, we have long forgotten their philosophy and values that gave us the Constitution we so ardently defend. John Locke was a major contributor to the philosophy and values encapsulated for posterity in their writings. It is time to dig into the soil of this treasure trove of material they took painstaking measures to preserve. When we unearth and reveal this treasure to a new generation, we honor our heritage and restore our inheritance.

---

76   Ibid, p. 30

10

Noah Webster's Magnum Opus

———— ◆◆◆◆◆ ————

*"The Bible must be considered as the great source of
all the truth by which men are to be guided in government
as well as in all social transactions."*

~ Noah Webster

An important unifying aspect of any culture is its
language. Colonial America emerged from the Revolutionary
War, established its new government, and yet still venerated
the King's English. Noah Webster's crowning achievement
would provide Americans a language of their own.

By the age of twenty-six, Webster had already published
his *Speller* for school children and a political tract entitled
Sketches of American Policy. This tract caught the eye of
General George Washington who issued an invitation to the
young Webster to visit him at Mount Vernon.

After dinner, Webster passionately expressed to General
Washington the need for national unity. He advocated the
benefits of a national, rather than state-oriented identity.
Webster had already begun to forge this new ground in his
Spellers which replaced British names of places with American
names.[77]

---

77 Kendall, Joshua. The Forgotten Founding Father Noah Webster's Obsession and the Creation of an
American Culture. Penguin Books, London, 2010, p. 3

Language, Webster believed, could be a tool of unification. This idea, only in seed form, would germinate in Webster until finally blossoming into his *American Dictionary.*

Webster would first languish trying to make a living as an attorney. Even then he was contributing to America. His eccentric, obsessive tendencies served the nation well. Whenever he visited a city, he would walk it and record a count of every house therein. This practice brought about the first American census in 1790. Moreover, his tenacious research into yellow fever helped organize "America's first medical journal and the field of public health."[78]

His achievements further included advancing female education and public schools, serving multiple terms in the Connecticut and Massachusetts state legislatures, establishing copyright law, and helping to found Amherst College. He also served as a successful newspaper editor, journalist, and political activist.[79]

In June of 1800, Webster writes in his newspaper, *The Connecticut Journal,* that he desires to write an American dictionary. The public is divided on the issue. At this time, Samuel Johnson, Jr.'s literary dictionary held public sway as the most authorized dictionary. Webster's proposed work would make Johnson's null and void.[80]

The innovative nature of his dictionary caused controversy. First, he would be creating a dictionary with a broader reach than for the purposes of literature. He would include scientific, medical, and geographic terms. However, the public outcry revolved around his intention to include everyday vocabulary of the American people, words never before entered into any dictionary. He would change the spelling of words, providing a standard spelling and making a distinction from that of the motherland.

---

78   Ibid, p. 6
79   Ibid, p. 6
80   Ibid, p. 231-232

Because of Webster, Americans spell "favor" instead of "favour" and "music" instead of "musick." He changed "centre" to "center" and legitimized distinctly American words like skunk, chowder, and hickory.

Seven years passed before Webster penned "A" upon a sheet of paper. Throughout 1807 he would work diligently, rising before dawn and working, while standing, until the sunlight waned for the day. He completed his work on "A" and "B" and then set aside the project for ten years.

1808 would bring a remarkable change to the Webster family. Pastor Moses Stuart, of New Haven's First Congregational Church, "began electrifying the entire town . . . and helped usher in . . . the Second Great Awakening."[81]

Webster's daughters influenced him to attend these revival meetings held by the new pastor. Following conversations with Pastor Stuart, Webster wrote, "Instead of obtaining peace, my mind was more and more disturbed." He wrestled with the weighty matter of his soul until, "A sudden impulse upon my mind arrested me . . . I instantly fell on my knees and confessed my sins to God, implored his pardon and made my vows to him and that I would live in entire obedience to his commands."[82]

Thereafter, the dictionary took on a new purpose. Previously the mission of any work he put his hands to was to make his mark on society. Webster's life, thus far, was a furious and continual attempt to achieve success. After his conversion, he saw the dictionary as a divine calling. Scripture now took on new meaning and would be incorporated into many of his definitions. Had his dictionary been completed before this conversion, America would have a very different lexicographic history.

An American Dictionary of the English Language prepared to meet the public in November 1828, hot off the press. Seventy thousand words painstakingly defined and legitimized

---

81 Ibid, p. 262

by Noah Webster entered American vocabulary. After decades of criticism by the press, *The Connecticut Mirror* printed this review: "We are aware of no other publication in this country or in Europe, upon which equal research and labor has ever been expended by a single individual."

Historian Joshua Kendall writes, "After Webster, all English lexicographers felt duty-bound to capture the language not just of literature, but also of everyday life."

The influence of Webster's faith is found throughout this great work as exampled below:[82]

---

educate

ED'UCATE, v.t. [L. educo, educare; e and duco, to lead.]

To bring up, as a child; to instruct; to inform and enlighten the understanding; to instill into the mind principles of arts, science, morals, religion and behavior. To educate children well is one of the most important duties of parents and guardians.

---

goodness

GOOD'NESS, n. The state of being good; the physical qualities which constitute value, excellence or perfection; as the goodness of timber, the goodness of a soil.

1. The moral qualities which constitute Christian excellence; moral virtue; religion. The fruit of the Spirit is love, joy peace, long-suffering, gentleness, goodness, faith, Gal. 5.

---

82   1828 Noah Webster Dictionary http://1828.mshaffer.com/

Noah Webster single-handedly provided America with a uniformed language distinctly Americanized complete with definitions borrowed from the greatest book of all time. It would seem the hand of Providence stayed the hand of Webster from completing this work prior to encountering the finished work of Christ. One could argue that the Second Great Awakening directly influenced the biblical nature of *Webster's Dictionary*. Revival spawned reformation, and yet with the passage of time, we are now at the crux of reformation once again.

While the Bible continues to define the nature of a nation, this nation no longer defines itself by the nature of the Bible. We call evil good and good evil. Perhaps it is time to return to the roots of our definitions. One man with pen and paper revolutionized a nation's language and gave it its own lingual heritage. Honoring this man's great work can restore the heritage that can redefine America.

11

William McGuffey and
the *McGuffey Eclectic Readers*

———————•◆◆◆•———————

*"Learning is not attained by chance; it must be sought for with
ardor and attended to with diligence."*

~ Abigail Adams

American children of the mid-nineteenth century were
essentially educated by the works of one man, William
Holmes McGuffey. The *McGuffey Eclectic Readers* sold 120
million copies between 1836 and 1920. These sales are
comparable only to the Bible and *Webster's Dictionary*.[83]

William Holmes McGuffey [1800-1873] began his
educational profession at the age of fourteen after receiving
a teaching certificate from his educator, Reverend William
Wick. As instructed, he put an advertisement in the local
paper that he would begin a four-month session of classes,
six days a week and eleven hours a day on the first day of
September 1814. Forty-eight students assembled from
the West Union, Ohio community, now Calcutta, Ohio.
McGuffey drew his lessons primarily from the Bible.[84]

---

83   Westerhoff, John H. III. *McGuffey and His Readers: Piety, Morality and Education in Nineteenth-
Century America.* Milford, Motts Media, Inc. 1982, p. 14.
84   Ibid. p. 32-33.

A traveling Presbyterian pastor took notice of McGuffey's teaching skills and offered to take him to reside in his home while he attended Old Stone Academy. McGuffey did so for the next four years. He then continued his education at Washington College for the next six years, where he taught, studied, and worked the farm to pay for his education. When he could not afford to buy his books, he copied them longhand. Before completing his degree, he received an offer to become a professor at Miami University in Oxford, Ohio. He accepted this position and held it for ten years before moving to Charlottesville, Virginia where he became a professor at the University of Virginia for twenty-eight years. Moreover, the Oxford Presbytery ordained McGuffey in 1829 as he loved to preach and demonstrated a superb ability to "communicate extemporaneously."[85]

McGuffey believed that children's textbooks were lacking efficiency in training children to read. Therefore, he began to assemble young children on his porch to experiment with how to best teach them to read. With the use of newspaper clippings and other collected writings, he created a curriculum best suited to their development. These sessions were the beginnings of what would become the *Eclectic Readers*.[86]

McGuffey's Readers focused on reading, elocution, rhetoric, and memorization. He accomplished this by instructing the child to read the provided story aloud and retell the story in his own words, either verbally or by writing it down. Then the child articulated the lesson learned or the moral of the story, thereby demonstrating his understanding of its meaning.[87] The *Readers* compiled reading material, prose, and poetry from American and English religious leaders as well as from George Washington, Thomas Jefferson, John Milton, William Shakespeare, Lord Byron, and Noah Webster to name a few.[88]

---

85   Ibid. p. 34-40.
86   Ibid. p. 45.
87   Ibid. p. 57-58.
88   Ibid. p. 59.

Bible narratives and quotations of Scripture were prominent throughout the *Readers*. Salvation and righteousness were central themes. Secondary themes were piety, kindness, and patriotism.[89] McGuffey adeptly weaved the values of loving God, your neighbor, and your country throughout his textbooks. Children were continually taught honesty, obedience, industry, cleanliness, forgiveness, gratefulness, cooperativeness, curiosity, self-control, meekness, independence, courageousness, frugality, punctuality, truthfulness, perseverance, responsibility, and honesty.[90]

The preface of the *Fourth Eclectic Reader* states:

From no source has the author drawn more copiously, in his selections, then from the sacred Scriptures. For this he certainly apprehends no censure. In a Christian country, that man is to be pitied, who at this day, can honestly object to imbuing the minds of youth with the language and spirit of the Word of God.[91]

The preface to the *Third Eclectic Reader* states:

The time has gone by, when any sensible man will be found to object to the Bible as a school book, in a Christian country, unless it be on purely sectarian principles, which should never find a place in systems of general education.[92]

And:

The Bible is the only book in the world treating of ethics and religion, which is not sectarian. Every sect claims that book as authority for its peculiar views.[93]

It was normal at the time of that writing to infer America to be a Christian nation and to consider the Bible the authority on educating in matters of morality and religion. The concern

---

89   Ibid. p. 91-92
90   Ibid. p. 94.
91   Ibid., p. 61
92   Ibid, p. 62
93   Ibid, p. 62

in that era was only to avoid promoting one sect over another, but central to all was the Bible. It was this idea that provided the stable foundation for America for centuries. It is a wholly modern American idea that the Bible ought to hold no position in the public education of children.

William McGuffey was only responsible for the original editions of the first four *Readers*. The fifth and sixth *Readers* were written by his brother Alexander McGuffey. Until 1941, the *Readers* were simply titled *Eclectic Readers*. It was not until later editions that they bore McGuffey's name in the title.[94] Nonetheless, the name did not signify continuity of content. Later editions contained revisions that greatly decreased the biblical and God-centered content of the original works of McGuffey.[95]

The greatest revisions are found in the 1879 edition, which is still available in print today. These books are the farthest from the original McGuffey content. Just the same, I own an 1865 printing of *McGuffey's Third New Eclectic Reader* and it is dramatically altered from the original 1837 printing. Where the original edition has essays on the *Character of Jesus, The Bible, More about the Bible, The Goodness of God, Gospel Invitation,* and *Character of Martin Luther*, the 1865 edition is lacking these entries.[96] The 1865 edition does contain The Lord's Prayer and A Child's Prayer.[97]

The later editions continued in the flavor of moral and civic responsibility instruction while significantly decreasing references to God and the Bible. Many Americans that were educated by the *McGuffey Readers* have fond recollections. Henry Ford reprinted the 1857 edition personally in 1928 due to his cherished memories of their use in his education.

---

94   Ibid, p. 21
95   Ibid, p. 17,19, 104-107
96   Ibid. p. 136 --137
97   McGuffey, William H., McGuffey's New Eclectic Third Reader. Ohio: Hinkle and Wilson, 1865.

He wrote:

> Most youngsters of my day were brought up on the
> *McGuffey Readers*. Most of those youngsters who still
> survive have a profound respect for the compiler of
> the *Readers*. The moral principles Dr. William Holmes
> McGuffey stressed, the solid character-building qualities
> he emphasized, are stressed and emphasized . . . today
> even though the *McGuffey Readers* themselves are not
> "required reading.[98]

Additionally, the *Saturday Evening Post* in 1927 ran an
article on McGuffey authored by Hugh Fullerton:

> For seventy-five years his [McGuffey's] system and his
> books guided the minds of four-fifths of the school
> children of the nation in their taste for literature, in
> their morality, in their social development and next to
> the Bible in their religion.[99]

In kind, Ralph Rush in his book *The Literature of the
Middle Western Frontier* wrote concerning McGuffey:

> Upon the generations immediately succeeding the
> pioneer period the influence of McGuffey may well have
> been greater than any other writer or statesman in the
> West. His name has become tradition not yet extinct.[100]

McGuffey provided the formative curriculum for the
new nation in the educational spirit of the Founding Fathers
who were greatly desirous of school teachers educating youth
in biblical morality and patriotic civic responsibility. They
believed that the success of this nation depended upon a
well-educated populace capable of governing themselves
and participating in the governing of the nation. McGuffey,
in his essay entitled *General Education*, thoroughly evinced
this necessity: "No thought is more true, and no truth

---

98 Westerhoff, John H. III. McGuffey and His Readers: Piety, Morality and Education in Nineteenth-Century America. Milford, Motts Media, Inc. 1982, p. 15.

99 Ibid. p. 15.

100 Ibid., p. 16.

more important, than that general intelligence is the only palladium of our free institutions."[101]

101   Ibid. p. 164.

12

The Wealth of a Nation

⚊⚊◆◆◆◆⚊⚊

*"What is prudence in the conduct of every private family can
scarce be folly in that of a great kingdom."*

~ Adam Smith

Americans have become the government's greatest
supporters. Conservatives portend to want the government
to do something about the economy as much as liberals do.
Perhaps when we see the government as the problem, it will
become easier to see it as the solution. Granted, a government
that has overstepped its proper boundaries of authority has
indeed become a problem, but the solution is not to sway that
intrusion to support one party's values over another. Rather,
it's to forbid the usurpation altogether.

Having a stable economy is one of the most necessary
ingredients to ensure the wealth and strength of a nation.
A free, industrious, and productive people are tantamount
to a stable economy. Adam Smith's *The Wealth of Nations*
is a comprehensive authority on the subject of national
economics. Published in 1776, it became the bedrock
philosophy of American economics. It became so not because
the Founders designed our economy after Smith's philosophy,
but because Smith meticulously envisioned a free market
society before it ever existed.[102] Reading Smith, it is easy to

---

102   Smith, Roy C. Adam Smith and the Origins of American Enterprise, Truman Talley Books.
New York, 2004

believe he merely described a free market society as it was, instead of theorizing something yet to be born on a national scale. Thus, we look to this Scottish moral philosopher not for a philosophy to impose, but to reimagine the vision of what is possible when a free and industrious people prosper.

Smith advised on the role of government in conjunction with a free and burgeoning economy. He writes, "Upon every account, therefore, the attention of government never was so unnecessarily employed as when directed to watch over the preservation or increase of the quantity of money in any country."[103] A free people are the engine that produces the economic stability of a nation. The engine is too massive a machine of industry to be monitored by any small entity of government. It requires the continual oil and energy of the entire community of all its parts to maintain stability.

Anytime one part of the machine is given favor over another through unnatural means, such as government involvement, it becomes off-kilter. The other parts have to work harder than their fair share, and the strain affects the favored portion as detrimentally as the unfavored. Smith explains, "To hurt in any degree the interest of any one order of citizens, for no other purpose but to promote that of some other, is evidently contrary to that justice and equality of treatment which the sovereign owes to all the different orders of his subjects."[104]

Smith writes, "But there is no country in which the whole annual produce is employed in maintaining the industrious. The idle everywhere consume a great part of it.[105]" He defines the idle as the disabled, the foolish, the elderly, the children, and those necessary industries that do not increase national production. Those in the last category provide services for the community such as doctors, nurses, and lawyers, but are not considered producers. All of these become, in essence,

---

103   Smith, Adam. The Wealth of Nations. Barnes & Noble. New York, 2004 (1776) p. 285
104   Ibid. p. 373
105   Ibid. p. 44

supported by those who are producing. Every person or group of people who are consuming or producing is of equal value in a free market society. Government regulation that favors the idle over the producers will hamper production and harm the idle. Regulation that favors the producers over the non-producing valuable renderers of services will harm the needs of the producers in the process.

Moreover, the government ought not to create jobs for the unemployed where society is not able to support the creation of said jobs. Smith argues, "No regulation of commerce can increase the quantity of industry in any society beyond what its capital can maintain."[106] If the engine of a nation's economy is not operating at the level at which it can expand to employ more workers, no regulations will overcome that reality. In contrast, freedom, over time, will naturally lend itself to an increase of capital for healthy businesses and will weed out the businesses that are not healthy.

Understanding the difficulty of assuming such a grandiose position as to rule and regulate economic affairs cautions a people towards such a one who would think himself capable of the task. Smith wrote this warning in 1776:

> The statesman, who should attempt to direct private people in what manner they ought to employ their capitals, would not only load himself with a most unnecessary attention, but assume an authority which could safely be trusted, not only to no single person, but to no council or senate whatever, and which would nowhere be so dangerous as in the hands of a man who had folly and presumption enough to fancy himself fit to exercise it.[107]

Furthermore, Smith writes:

> The sovereign is completely discharged from a duty, in the attempting to perform which he must always be

106   Ibid. p. 298
107   Ibid. p. 300

exposed to innumerable delusions, and for the proper performance of which no human wisdom or knowledge could ever be sufficient; the duty of superintending the industry of private people and of directing it towards the employments most suitable to the interest of society.[108]

The government does provide a valuable service to the national economy in three areas for which its authority is relegated. The first is in defending against foreign invasion by maintaining a regulated military. The second is protecting its citizenry from each other by maintaining a justice system. And lastly, to maintain the public works common to the needs of all citizenry, such as roads, bridges, and canals. Each of these services requires a portion of the common produce of the nation, acquired through taxation. Moreover, the object of a government supportive of a healthy national economy is to keep as much of the people's capital in their own pockets as possible. In so doing, this increases the continued revenue drawn from taxation, as that capital is put to productive use by the people.[109]

Adam Smith is an avid proponent of a free market economy. When each portion of the economy is working to produce in alignment with their own interest, the interests of the other portions are maintained. He writes, "All systems either of preference or of restraint, therefore, being thus completely taken away, the obvious and simple system of natural liberty establishes itself of its own accord. Every man, as long as he does not violate the laws of justice, is left perfectly free to pursue his own interest his own way, and to bring both his industry and capital into competition with those of any other men, or order of men."[110]

Even if the economic engine were to falter due to any of the numerous pressures being applied to it, a free, knowledgeable, and industrious people can reignite the

---

108   Ibid. p. 399
109   Ibid. p. 419-420
110   Ibid. p. 399

economic engine. Those who did not build on a firm foundation would be in a more difficult situation than those who did. Thus, some will feel the jolt of the engine grinding to a stop and subsequently restarting more than others. We need not be victims of an economic shift, but rather a people who can position ourselves appropriately towards economic progress. Smith argues that if a society were to no longer have money to exchange for goods and services, that it would barter, "though with a good deal of inconveniency,"[111] until a trustworthy currency was reestablished.

At whatever stage an economy may be, the healthy thing to do is to increase the capital of the society through productive enterprise. Where capital is lacking, "parsimony, and not industry is the immediate cause of the increase of capital."[112] Frugal saving of one's money or goods is primary before sowing that accrued capital into a productive endeavor, which reaps a greater return. Industry can only produce more of something that already exists. It takes the five loaves of bread and makes them multiply to feed five thousand; it doesn't make five loaves of bread appear out of thin air.[113]

When we are positioned in a way that we are not consuming all our capital, but creating capital through stewardship of our resources, we will be able to apply that knowledge regardless of our national circumstances. If we are ignorant of the system and our dependence upon it, we will feel our world has crashed instead of realizing that we are the gears of the economic system. When we each live life in a way that is appropriately balanced in how we manage our own affairs and businesses, we are contributing to the whole. In contrast, when we live recklessly in terms of finances or in the way we do business, we contribute to the economic decline.

When we blame government, we absolve ourselves of our proper responsibility as the people of these United States.

---

111   Ibid. p. 285
112   Ibid. p. 233
113   Matthew 14:18

We become the victims, and the government, whom we consider to be the perpetrator, steals not only our economic prowess but also our identity as responsible citizens. The stealing happens because we see ourselves as helpless victims petitioning an all-powerful entity to fix our problems instead of being the problem-solvers. There are problems at the governmental level. We would have to be blind not to recognize that. But to hoist the entire system on the shoulders of an institution not designed to bear the burden is to further endanger the economic system.

The American people are designed to advance economic prosperity. To make a difference, we can learn how to be citizens that contribute to our national prosperity starting in our own homes, and then in the larger circles where we have influence. Owning the problem is the first step to becoming the solution. The national economy begins and ends with the people, and if it ends, it shall begin again with the people.

13

A Doctrine of Property

⟶ ◆◆◆ ⟵

"If history could teach us anything, it would be that private property is inextricably linked with civilization"

~ Ludwig von Mises

Jefferson penned the famous line encapsulating American freedom as the right to "life, liberty, and the pursuit of happiness." Time has eroded the meaning Jefferson sought to employ with the words "pursuit of happiness." History professes that Jefferson almost certainly borrowed the idea embodied in this phrase from George Mason's *Virginia Declaration of Rights,* May 1776:

> That all men are born equally free and independent, and have certain inherent natural Rights... among which are the Enjoyment of Life and Liberty, with the Means of acquiring and possessing Property, and pursuing and obtaining Happiness and Safety.

Moreover, Mason's conceptualization of the right to property and pursuit of happiness is traced directly to John Locke's philosophy.[114]

Locke argued that the land of the earth was given in common to man through Adam. He reasoned that in order

---

114 George Mason Bio. http://www.gunstonhall.org/georgemason/

to occupy such land, it would need to be cultivated by the labor of individual people. The fruit of such labor would then belong to the laborer for he will have added his own work to nature and could then claim the result as his own. Thus, the land he worked would be his to work. The produce he harvested would be his to harvest, keep, trade, give, or sell. His ownership would be directly related to that which he occupied by his labor.

The role of government then is to protect those borders of a person's property. A person's pursuit of happiness is ensconced in his ability to be free to labor and steward the fruits of his labor.[115] Locke argues: "But because no political society can be, nor subsist, without having in itself the power to preserve the property . . . [116] Here he is explaining that a political society must be able to protect the property of its members. For this idea of property requires the institution of moral and physical boundaries to a person's property. To have a right to have property indelibly means that your land or personal items are yours and yours alone, and not also another person's.

The Ten Commandments were given in a context of community where stealing could not be permitted. For something to be stolen, it has to belong to one person and not another. In the same way, for something to be given it has to belong to the giver to be received as a blessing by the receiver. If the labor of individuals belongs to everyone in common, no one is ever stealing and no one is ever giving, nor is anyone practicing stewardship. Labor becomes forced, and the workers must work for more than themselves for society to continue.

---

115   Locke, John. *Second Treatise of Government.* Barnes and Noble: New York, 1690 and 2004, Chapter 5.
116   Ibid., Chapter 7.

In keeping with the 8ᵗʰ and 10ᵗʰ Commandments forbidding the stealing and coveting of property, Locke implores that:

> Man being born, as has been proved, with a title to perfect freedom, and an uncontrolled enjoyment of all the rights and privileges of the law of nature, equally with any other man, or number of men in the world, hath by nature a power, not only to preserve his property, that is, his life, liberty and estate, against the injuries and attempts of other men; but to judge of, and punish the breaches of that law in others, as he is persuaded the offence deserve . . .

Here is where we have the institution of government to protect the liberty of a people joined together as a nation. A nation's government then has a moral duty to uphold the right of the people to their own property. People are then entitled to the property they own rather than the property owned by others.

One of the earliest American colonies learned the hard way that working a jointly owned land and subsequent harvest would not produce enough food for the community. The fallen nature of man created those who simply refused to do their fair share of work, and the remaining workers could not do enough to cover their slack. The harvest was insufficient to feed the community and many starved during the winter months including women and children. Everyone wanted to eat of the food produced by a few, so the few suffered along with the many. Captain John Smith decided this could not continue and declared "the labors of thirty or forty honest and industrious men shall not be consumed to maintain a hundred and fifty idle loiterers." Therefore, he invoked the teaching of the Apostle Paul and made the ruling declaration that if you do not work you will not eat. He then gave each family their own plot of land to steward, solving the problem of their starvation. Now they would be responsible to labor for their own sustenance.[117]

Americans take for granted this concept of property. We have created a modernized meaning to "the pursuit of happiness." What we pursue is the benefits of another person's labor, rather than enjoying the freedom to produce our own property. We demand happiness rather than create it. This has become a national problem because it is first a family problem. Many parents give their children everything without any boundaries or responsibilities. They don't want to see them suffer to work hard for something, nor do they want them to suffer with the results of not working. In an attempt to protect them from hardship, they remove the boundaries of their labor allowing it to be sucked dry by the desires of their children. They sacrifice for their children where their children will not sacrifice for themselves.

When the reservoirs are depleted the children, now adults, look for the next well to tap into—the government. The right to pursue happiness has now trampled on the right to property because the seekers of happiness trample on the owners of property. Property is no longer sacred. It is plundered and redistributed to create happiness for those who cannot maintain it.

Many Americans have bought into entitlement—the idea that they are due a portion of the labor of others. This is not a new way of thinking. However, the strange phenomena are those who no longer see their property as their own. The boundaries of what belongs to them and what belongs to another do not exist. Their property is neither stolen nor

---

117 Montgomery, Denise. *Captain John Smith*. The Colonial Williamsburg Foundation. http://www.history.org/foundation/journal/smith.cfm

given. It is simply no longer personally owned, but rather communally consumed. There is no violation because there is no ownership. In a sense, the laborer is a slave to the consumer, and the consumer is responsible to no one. We cannot practice loving our neighbor because there is no distinction between me and my neighbor.

Jesus said to those who have, more shall be given, but to those who do not have, even the little they have shall be taken.[118] This is because there are those who are able to have because they understand the creation and stewardship of property, but there are those who have no such understanding. These unfortunate people cannot keep anything, for it all slips through their fingers as they consume it. Some have trouble even consuming what they are given, for without boundaries it is lost to them before it reaches their needs.

Without a philosophy of the right to property, a society cannot maintain the economic structure necessary for a free people. Soon those who have will rule those who have not because the difference in culture will be too staggering to reverse. A government of freedom will have to give way to a government of control to manage the people who cannot manage themselves. If a man without self-control is like a city without walls,[119] consider what a community of people without self-control will be like. We cannot remove boundaries of property to help people. We have to help within the construct of them being responsible for themselves. We increase the problem as soon as we remove the boundaries. Their problem becomes our problem. Instead of getting closer to solving it, we become part of their problem. The right of property is, therefore, indispensable to a free people.

---

118 Matthew 13:12
119 Proverbs 25:28

14

Sustaining Capitalism

———◆◆◆◆◆———

*"To think theologically about economics is, first of all,
to learn some economics."*

~ Michael Novak

The Medieval era has long held a hidden picture of what
Christian creativity and innovation look like. The Christian
society that flourished after the collapse of Rome invented
and produced in a way the world had never seen before. They
harnessed the power of the horse, invented the printing press,
the wheelbarrow, eyeglasses, wagons, astronomy, science,
weapons of war, and fish farming. What is more, they
invented the clock so that people could tell time and organize
their day for more efficient use of their time. Prior to the
clock they only had the church bell to signal the approximate
time at certain intervals in a day.[120]

These inventions reduced manual labor and increased
productivity and profits. This generated wealth that was
then used as capital to produce more. Thus, capitalism
was birthed. Only some areas of Europe flourished into
a capitalistic economy and then declined. The Protestant
Reformation brought a rebirth to innovation and creativity

---

120   Stark, Rodney. Victory of Reason. New York; Random House, 2005, p 33-68.

that spread over into the New World.

A capitalistic society is a byproduct of certain conditions only present in a free society born out of the Christian worldview. It is not merely the freedom to make money and keep it or use it for whatever one likes. It is the flourishing of people who are innovatively producing goods and services, and using the values produced to generate more. Capitalism is practiced when people are free to use their God-given ingenuity to produce a harvest from which a portion is sown again into continued reproduction.

Several key elements are crucial to sustain such an economy. Security of personal property is a necessary first development of a capitalistic society. If people are fighting to protect what they have from thieves or high taxes, they lack the stability to produce and steward their production. Instead they will hide, hoard, or under produce to limit the property they must protect. Only in a society where personal property is protected by law will people feel safe enough to move from surviving to flourishing.

Innovation is the next indispensable ingredient to a capitalistic economy. Once property is secure, people will use ingenuity and creativity to find easier ways to produce, which in turn creates inventions to ease production and increase the ability for others to produce. For instance, only in Christianized Medieval Europe did the ability to produce paper create the desire for a greater method of manufacturing books. The invention of the printing press increased the ability of writers to produce literature, which increased the desire for learning, thereby benefiting education.[121] All of this generated the production of book binders, ink, and newspapers. It's kingdom increase.

When we see capitalism as an "ism"—a philosophy to be imposed on a society—we fail to create the bedrock necessary to sustain it. It is not an "ism" like Socialism, Marxism, and

---

121   Ibid, p. 39.

Communism. It requires these elements of society that are only found in a Christian society. As the Christian worldview slips, it is only natural that capitalism is less sustainable.

A consumer economy will not serve this end. The idea of "disposable" income is antithetical to the thinking that produces capitalistic increase. One does not need to be a business owner to be a capitalist, nor are all business owners' capitalists. If the person does not sow their produced wealth into the ground to make more, they are not practicing capitalism. The people who produce and use their production as capital to increase their gains are capitalists. A worker who works for wages, and uses those wages to reinvest for gains, is practicing capitalism. The worker or employer who consumes his or her earnings is not practicing capitalism or helping to sustain the economy.

If society wants goods and services that are produced at low quality and great quantity for fast consumption, they fail to create an economy of innovation. Why create something excellent if people are happy with mediocrity? People are consuming their capital when they expend their resources on goods and services that do not hold up with time and usage.

American Christians are looking for what they can do to stabilize an economy. But often we are not looking in the right places. We look for how we can change a system, not how we can change our own living. Some will influence a system, but many will be most effective starting with their own finances.

Capitalism, like anything else, has extremes to avoid. Big businesses that make massive amounts of wealth and pay their employees only enough to eke out a living are not aiding a healthy economy. Stifling health care laws and tax burdens cause business owners to take self-preservation measures that hinder the ability of their workers to flourish. Such conditions are not tantamount to production and innovation. Colonial American manufacturers had to pay their employees high wages to compete with their ample ability to start their own business and enjoy their own profits. This created incentive for greater innovation as people raced to find solutions to reduce the need for labor workers so that they could reinvest resources for greater profits.[122]

Most importantly, the last essential element to creating and sustaining a capitalistic economy is a Christian worldview. Only in a world where man can have dominion over the earth rather than be a victim of the earth can the conditions be right for innovation and production. In many worldviews, time is dominate over man and man is at its mercy. In Christianized Europe, man developed a way to use time for his purposes, just as he invented a way to use the horse for his purposes. Only in a Christian worldview is the idea of private property sustainable. If what I produce belongs equally to you, why would I produce it to be consumed by you? Or if what I earn is taken by high taxes, why would I work harder to make more? Only in Judeo-Christian ethics is personal property not to be stolen or coveted. It is in this worldview that a person has responsibility to grow what they have into more.

In light of these ideas, consider the verse Matthew 25:29: **"For to everyone who has, more shall be given, and he will have an abundance; but from the one who does not have, even what he does have shall be taken away."** We can apply this to economics. Those who have more shall be given more. If they cannot keep what they have, they cannot do with more. If they do not have the ability to keep anything, even what they produce will be taken.

In America, the economic problems not only include government encroachment on personal property and the ability to produce more, but a worldview of economic equality where people want what belongs to another. Moreover, this worldview includes those who want people to have access to what belongs to them. Socialism is not only being imposed by government; it is being home-grown

---

122   Ibid, p. 222-225.

amongst the citizenry. The lines of personal property are being blurred to where justice is served when all who have need partake from all who have resources. To protect one's property is seen as unjust, and maybe even un-Christian. The problem is that when people take from the production of others, their resources are consumed and are not reinvested. The economy cannot maintain that kind of stress. The givers and the takers will pay that price if this mentality is not corrected.

Lastly, for those who still have a healthy view of personal property, there is danger in maintaining a prolonged defense to protect that property. The methods of defense often are contrary to the environment necessary for innovation and production. Setting one's mind on self-preservation often creates a lack of generosity, as well as hoarding, hiding, and under producing as discussed above. Christians and concerned citizens who wish to aid economic progress will need to balance their decisions with love for their neighbor, and thus their nation. This will require creative, God-inspired thinking to avoid the pitfalls of protecting one's own property and continuing to practice free enterprise.

It can be done. It has been done. Christians have stabilized economies before, and we can do it again. The Bible says that the wealth of the wicked is stored up for the righteous. If we live from another kingdom, thereby practicing kingdom economics, we will produce results in our nation. The kingdom of God will be demonstrated, and the world will ask where our hope is coming from as our finances and businesses flourish despite the natural conditions. Then we will be able to answer that our hope comes from Christ Jesus.

15

Theology of Nations, Part I

"Biblical nationalism was different from Germany's secular nationalism. The former was God-centered rather than culture-or race-centered. Being a product of God's promise and law, it had to remain self-critical and repentant. Old Testament characters like Moses, Daniel, Nehemiah, and several of the prophets powerfully exhibited this peculiar, repentant nationalism."

~ Vishal Mangalwadi

We have lost our theology. America has lost the theology that built great nations. Reformers labored to create it. Many have given their lives to protect it. Yet it has become buried in the annals of church history. The foundational pillars of American government are rooted in Protestant theology, and some are found specifically in the theology of John Calvin.

Until recently, I associated Calvin only with doctrines on predestination. Even though I knew him to be a major player in the Protestant Reformation, I had no idea the scope of his contribution to America. This all changed when I read Abraham Kuyper's *Lectures on Calvinism* which were delivered to Princeton University in 1898.

Dutch journalist and theologian, Abraham Kuyper, challenged his audience to dig into the foundational principles of the Reformation that created free nations. Kuyper illustrated that Calvinism developed philosophy on every area of life.

Calvin did not restrain his theology to matters of the spirit but extended it to the practical:

> Only of Calvinism can it be said that it has consistently and logically followed out the lines of the Reformation, has established not only Churches but also States, has set its stamp upon social and public life, and has thus, in the full sense of the word, created for the whole life of man a world of thought entirely its own.[123]

Calvin gave nations the doctrine of the sovereignty of God. The Bible gave us the truth of this doctrine, but Calvin thought it out and applied it. He gave us a template for the congruous outworking of the state, the church, and the people. In modern times, we debate the topic of separation of church and state. We think it a modern issue, but the answer to our debate lies in our history.

Calvin taught that God is sovereign over the church, God is sovereign over the state, and God is sovereign over the people (families, individuals, and the outworking of culture such as science, art, entertainment, and business). Thus, separation of church and state is not separation of God and state. In fact, "the sovereignty of the state and the sovereignty of the church exist side by side, and they mutually limit each other."[124] The church has no jurisdiction over the government, nor does the government have authority over the church. But God has authority over both.

If we do not understand our history, we are in danger of wanting the church to rule the nation. Instead, we want a church that operates as a church and not the state. God's sovereignty over the state does not open the door for the

---

123   Kuyper, Abraham. Lectures on Calvinism., USA:ReadaClassic.com, 2010. p. 145
124   Kuyper, p. 79

church to encroach on the state. Nor can either entity control the freedom of the people. We cannot dominate culture the way the world does. Our job is to change culture without using worldly weapons. Even non-violent methods of coercion are worldly weapons. We don't coerce. We transform. Transformation will bring reformation if our theology provides for it. But the world will dominate any area of life that the church has no use for.

Even though we are a nation whose government is for the people and by the people, we cannot lean so far right that the voice of the people nullifies the voice of the government. If the people are completely sovereign over the state, we will have anarchy. Even though we are a nation with a strong federal government, we cannot lean so far to the left that the voice of the government nullifies the voice of the people. The people are to be freely sovereign under God without usurping the healthy mandate of a government. Each group ought to work together in proper tension to each other.

As Christians, it is normal to want our way of life to be supreme in the land. The more we align with the Bible, the healthier our nation will be. The problem is in how we accomplish this goal. It will not serve us in the long run for the church to demand power over the government, even to bring good correction to it. If we do not understand the structure of our nation we can, in our ignorance, make matters worse, rather than better. When we think we would be better off without government, we lose sight of what it means to be a nation. We cannot look at only how the government appears now, but at what it was designed to be.

Martin Luther was indispensable to the Reformation. Without Luther we would not have Calvin, but "Luther never worked out his fundamental thought."[125] In contrast, Calvin

---

125   Kuyper p. 145

developed an entire system that applies to government, church, science, family, business, etc. The sovereignty of God was not simply a doctrine for the church, but for the world. It was not left to the upper room of theology. Calvinists lived theology and built nations with it. No area of life was left bereft of theology. We have heard of applied sciences: this is applied theology.

If we do not have a theology for what a great nation looks like, we will not know where we are or where we are going. If our theology does not inform our politics, our thoughts will be informed by other groups that claim to represent our desires. We will not know if these groups truly represent us or not, because we do not have a theology that informs our thinking about our nation. Our theology should inform our politics more than our politics informs our theology. When we align completely with one political party, we have likely become absorbed by its worldview instead of doing the hard work of applying theology to the issues we face as a nation.

Kuyper spoke these words over one hundred years ago:

> Since Calvinism arose, not from an abstract system, but from life itself, it never was in the century of its prime presented as a systematic whole. The tree blossomed and yielded its fruit, but without anyone having made a botanic study of its nature and growth. Calvinism, in its rise, rather acted than argued. But now this study may no longer be delayed. [126]

Free nations do not just happen. It takes good theology to build great nations. G.K. Chesterton wrote that "philosophy is merely thought that has been thought out." Calvin has gifted America with theology which has been thought out and applied in such a manner that we no longer realize we are living within its branches.

---

[126] Kuyper p. 148

16

Theology of Nations, Part II

"God created the nations. They exist for Him."

~ Abraham Kuyper

Government is God's idea. When God called Abraham, He told him **"I will make nations of you, and kings will come forth from you."**[127] God repeated this over Sarah, **"I will bless her so that she will be the mother of nations; kings of peoples will come from her."**[128] Again God declares this over Jacob when He commissions him as Israel, **"And God said to him, 'I am God Almighty; be fruitful and increase in number. A nation and a community of nations will come from you, and kings shall come forth from you.'"**[129]

If nations with kings were God's intention, what about Saul?

"The Lord said to Samuel, "Listen to the voice of the people in regard to all that they say to you, for they have not rejected you, but they have rejected Me from being king over them. Like all the deeds which they have done since the day that I brought them up from Egypt even to this day—in that they have forsaken Me and served other

---

127   Genesis 17:6
128   Genesis 17:16
129   Genesis 35:11

gods—so they are doing to you also. Now then, listen to
their voice; however, you shall solemnly warn them and
tell them of the procedure of the king who will reign over
them" (I Samuel 8: 7-9).

Why were the people rejecting God by wanting a king?
Samuel proceeds to list the ways that this king will be a burden
to them. People have interpreted this passage as evidence that
government is not God's intention. However, we do not create
doctrine against government based on this passage because it was
God's response to a particular instance of the people demanding
a king rather than God's response to kings in general.

Kings were God's plan, but Saul was not. The problem
was not with the institution, but with the individual. Saul
was anointed to rule because the people demanded a king.
Otherwise, we would see this prophecy fulfilled for the first
time in David. Saul was an Ishmael. David was God's Isaac.
We do not look at Ishmael for God's intended prophetic
fulfillment, we look at Isaac. We do not look at God's response
to Saul as God's thoughts about kings and governments of
nations, we look at David.

David is in the lineage of Abraham, Isaac, and Jacob.
From David's line comes Jesus. Isaiah writes of Jesus, **"for a
child shall be born to us, a son will be given to us, and the
government will rest on his shoulders."**[130] God promised
that the **"throne of David will be established before the
Lord forever."**[131]

Paul writes, **"Every person is to be in subjection to the
governing authorities. For there is no authority except from
God, and those which exist are established by God."**[132]

---

130   Isaiah 9:6
131   I Kings 2:45
132   Romans 13:1

Saul could not have gained his authority without God establishing him. David submits to that authority, to the one who throws spears at him, even though he is rightly anointed as king. God brings Saul right into David's grasp, and David laments that he cut Saul's garment. When Saul is killed, David grieves his loss, rather than rejoicing that he is now to assume his kingship.

God's word never returns void. He did not promise Abraham nations and kings only to do away with them when Jesus comes with His kingdom. Jesus commissioned us to disciple nations, and this commissioning is in the context of the entire narrative of Scripture. John writes in Revelation that, "**the leaves of the tree are for the healing of the nations**."[133] God designed us to have healthy nations. Abraham is in the hall of faith[134] awaiting the fulfillment of God's promise. We partner with Abraham, Sarah, Isaac, and Jacob when we disciple nations and bring the healing that Jesus gained on the cross to each and every one of them.

Nations will change. They will come and go. Many nations we have today did not exist in Bible times, and many that did do not exist today. But we do know that God intends for nations to exist in a form that its people are subject to the leader or leaders of that nation. When we stray away from this form, we stray away from the truth.

In America, we live in the tension between two political perspectives. We are either leaning towards big government or we lean back the other way towards limited government. The constant tug of war keeps us from diving into the dangerous ditch on either side. It is just as important that we avoid the ditch of anarchy as it is to fall into the ditch of tyranny. We are a nation of the people, by the people, but it is the people

133   Revelation 22:2
134   Hebrews 11

united under a Constitution that includes each important part of the government. Sometimes we infer that government of the people is each person, or the people disunited with our various agendas. But it is a whole ship operating together as a unit. If any one-part gains too much power, the whole system is in jeopardy. Even the people having too much power can sink the ship.

When we see abuses of power, we tend to over-correct our course. We throw ourselves into a different error from the one we were avoiding. We watch Christians seek to strong arm the government to change culture, and we argue that we do not need to concern ourselves with matters of government because Jesus did not use political power. Consequently, we fall into another error. God does have a role for government, it just is not that one.

We do not use governmental power to transform a nation, but a transformed nation will have a transformed government. There is a difference between the church trying to disciple the nation through political power, and the government being discipled with truth as part of discipling the nation. We err when we believe that we must finagle the government to be an arm of the church. We also err when we think God's truth does not extend to our government.

Section III:
Reforming America

17

The Reformation

---

*"It was the Judeo-Christian tradition that had produced enough
integration of the disparate cultural elements of European
society to allow us to speak of a Western civilization easily
distinguishable from the Islamic world or even from Byzantium."*

~Willis Glover

Two of the greatest cultural shifts in human history hung
on a nail. The second event rests on the preeminence of the
first. These two events are the crucifixion of our Lord and
Martin Luther's nailing of the 95 Theses to the door of the
Wittenberg church in 1517. The Reformation resurrected the
Bible in a way that changed the world.

We greatly err if we relegate the Reformation to church
history rather than world history. It not only launched
reformation within the Catholic Church, and its own separate
and unstoppable church movement that revolutionized
Christianity thereafter, but it produced reformation of the
world itself. It made empires into nations and subjects into
citizens. It gave birth to governments, nations, written
languages, and a plethora of books, public education, modern
universities, science, hospitals, numerous businesses, and
innovations in every place it spread.

The power of the Reformation lay in its simplicity. It made the Bible the center of its movement. The Western world shifted from Christendom to kingdom. Truth brought liberty. America is "the great land of liberty" because she was first the great land of truth. America's foundational political philosophy is essentially applied theology as taught by the Reformers.

Francis Schaeffer wrote in *The Great Evangelical Disaster* in 1984:

> The Reformation with its emphasis upon the Bible, in all that it teaches, as being the revelation of God, provided a freedom in society and yet a form in society as well. Thus, there were freedoms in the Reformation countries (such as the world had never known before) without these freedoms leading to chaos—because both laws and morals were surrounded by a consensus resting upon what the Bible taught. . . We who are Bible-believing Christians no longer represent the prevailing moral outlook of our society, and no longer have the major influence shaping this.[135]

When we lose the theology of the Reformation, we lose the benefits along with it. We move from Christian to post-Christian, and eventually, to paganism. The theology of the Bible is not just for our churches, it is for our nations. Luther and Calvin gave us vocation. The doctrine of the priesthood of all believers meant that all people fulfilled the Lord's work on the earth. All people needed to be educated in the truth, not just the privileged.

Vishal Mangalwadi wrote in *The Book that Made Your World*:

> Education was a Christian missionary enterprise. It was integral to Christian missions because modern education is a fruit of the Bible. The biblical Reformation, born in European universities, took education out of the cloister and spread it around the globe.[136]

---

135 Schaeffer, Francis. *The Great Evangelical Disaster* (Wheaton: Crossway Books, 1984) p. 47-48

136 Mangalwadi, Vishal. *The Book that Made Your World*, United States: Thomas Nelson. 2011 p. 194

The soaring pulpits we see in historic Protestant churches were a testimony to the shift towards the authority of Scripture. The Protestant church came under the authority of Scripture, instead of the church being the authority over Scripture. Scripture applied to leaders and laity alike.

What began as a protest became a process that changed the world. It was never Luther's intention to start a new separate church movement. He only sought to deal with the issues of the church of his day in light of Scripture. But once the flame of truth shined brightly, he could not put it out. Facing death, he proclaimed "Here I stand, I can do no other."

Today, we stand, but we have forgotten how we got here. We decry nationhood as if it were the enemy of freedom, rather than its protector. We do not know life before the Reformation. No living person does. There is no one to give us an *It's a Wonderful Life* experience where we see our world without Martin Luther. Martin Luther has left his indelible stamp upon it. What we believe to be common is uncommon. It is a world shaped by biblical revelation that now believes it has always thought this way.

Lest we all forget, let us learn again to stand on the truth of Scripture, not only for our salvation, but for our nation. The bedrock of American government is not found in Greek literature, but in Hebrew and Greek Scriptures. It is not found on Mount Olympus, but on Mount Sinai. Russel Kirk wrote in his book, *The Roots of American Order,* that "In the beginning, America was Protestant: that point has been emphasized by every historian of the United States."[137]

America owes a huge debt of gratitude to Martin Luther. Without the Reformation, there would be no land of liberty. Celebrating the anniversary of the Protestant Reformation is as important as celebrating Independence Day. Without Reformation Day, there would be no Independence Day.

---

137   Kirk, Russel. *Roots of American Order* (Washington, DC: Regnery, 1991) p. 229

The key to restoring America, or any nation, is the truth of the Bible becoming central once again. Luther read the Bible and changed the world. Luther taught that "the Bible is the cradle wherein Christ is laid." To disciple our world in Christ is to lay the foundation of Scripture.

That foundation is deep in the bedrock of our nation. Our job is to unearth it once again. The theological work has been done by the Reformers. They gave us that gift, but somewhere the baton dropped. The Bible, as the handbook of truth for the world, became merely the handbook of faith for the church. It is time to carry the legacy the of the Reformers forward. Let us be the reformers of our day so that we guarantee that our land remains one of liberty.

18

The Thinking of Tyranny

<hr />

"The only basis for genuine human rights and dignity is a fully biblical worldview."

~ Nancy Pearcey

The forethought the Founding Fathers encapsulated into the Constitution is astounding. They securely embedded protection of the people's liberty into the very framework of government. The Founders took meticulous care to avoid future subversion of those liberties from foes both foreign and domestic. Success in undermining this carefully formed Republic would require an evil genius mastermind, or a silent foe of another kind.

Tyranny does not require a tyrant as much as it requires the loss of a worldview that sustains liberty. The Constitution expressly divides the powers of government into three separate branches: Executive, Legislative, and Judicial. It further divides the Legislative into two parts: the Congress and the Senate. Before the Constitution was ratified, some states, especially New York, maintained concern that a powerful federal government would usurp the power of the states. The Father of the Constitution, James Madison, argued profusely for the soundness of the Constitution in the *Federalist Papers*.

Madison reminded the dissenters that the balance of power was not merely between the state governments and the federal government, but between the powerful people and both institutions of government.

Madison professed that the three separate powers of the federal government would have to succeed in tyrannically uniting and commanding the military force against the nation. Then the states would have to fail to rise up and overthrow such tyranny. Provided this most extraordinary event, he was confident that the people would organize private militia to swiftly and successfully squelch the tyranny.[138] Madison composed these thoughts shortly after the Revolutionary War. The people had already done this very thing when they declared their independence from Great Britain.

The Federalist Papers #46 written by James Madison provides eloquent clarity on this subject. Should the federal government exceed its proper legal jurisdiction and encroach upon the rights of the people, Madison writes:

> The disquietude of the people; their repugnance and, perhaps, refusal to co-operate with the officers of the Union; the frowns of the executive magistracy of the State; the embarrassments created by legislative devices, which would often be added on such occasions, would oppose, in any State, difficulties not to be despised; would form, in a large State, very serious impediments; and where the sentiments of several adjoining States happened to be in unison, would present obstructions which the federal government would hardly be willing to encounter.

> But ambitious encroachments of the federal government, on the authority of the State governments, would not excite the opposition of a single State, or of a few States

---

138   Madison, James. *The Federalist Papers* # 46 & #47, Penguin Books: New York, p. 294-308

only. They would be signals of general alarm. Every government would espouse the common cause. A correspondence would be opened. Plans of resistance would be concerted. One spirit would animate and conduct the whole. The same combinations, in short, would result from an apprehension of the federal, as was produced by the dread of a foreign, yoke; and unless the projected innovations should be voluntarily renounced, the same appeal to a trial of force would be made in the one case as was made in the other. But what degree of madness could ever drive the federal government to such an extremity.[139]

If the people are protected to such an extent that Madison considered it madness for the federal government to even attempt such an encroachment, why is it now possible for the Executive Branch to supersede the authority of the Legislative Branch? Why do we have a Supreme Court that is overruling the state courts in sweeping decisions? Why do people argue that there is a great conspiracy at work undermining the liberty of the people of these United States? The Constitution was built to withstand such a plan. However, there could be a foe that the Founders could not counter by matter of law.

John Adams wisely opined that "Our Constitution was made only for a moral and religious people. It is wholly inadequate to the government of any other."[140] The Founders knew that a free nation could not make Christianity a matter of law, but they advocated the people be perpetually educated in the Bible so as to safeguard our liberty.

What we are now calling "conspiracy" or "indoctrination" is the predominance of a way of thinking that is no longer

---

139   Madison, James. The Federalist Papers # 46, Penguin Books: New York, p. 294-300.

140   Adams, John (President) to the Officers of the First Brigade of the Third Division of the Militia of Massachusetts, 1798 http://johnadamscenter.com/who-we-are/why-john-adams/

biblical. It is a secular offshoot of Christianity that is losing all resemblance of its parentage.

Our foe is not a President or a political party, but a worldview. America has lost the Christian worldview that esteems truth, justice, honor, responsibility, honesty, servility, humility, and hard work, etc. No one stole these biblical precepts from our nation; they fell by the wayside. They are the casualties of our failure to disciple our nation. When the American Christians became more interested in avoiding the world than cultivating a functioning nation, we lost precious cargo we once carried. We built a weak subculture instead of a strong national culture.

Why do we see the warning signs of tyranny? We see this because we did not help maintain a culture that sustains liberty. We abdicated our role in culture and left it to grow its own worldview. It grew into something we do not recognize and has firmly snaked its way into all spheres of culture. Now that we see its effects we are crying out, but we wrongly want to deal with the people embodying the worldview. We do not realize that the same worldview is predominate across the spectrum, and that we cannot fight it by fighting people.

It is not that Americans will not elect a Christian President because they do not want God in their country. Americans do not want a Christian President because he or she is foreign to their worldview, and they fear what this outsider may bring. We are still trying to respond to the culture like it is a backsliding Christian culture, instead of a wholly secular culture. We take assaults on Christianity like an anti-religious attack against God instead of a cultural reaction to a foreign worldview. The Christian worldview has become the foreigner.

Failing to understand this will be our undoing. Francis Schaefer argued that we were facing "a rapidly changing cultural situation" and that if we didn't understand the culture our message would fall "on deaf ears."[141]

We are a people who live in the light, and that light is more powerful than any darkness no matter how great the void. We have dulled our swords taking swings at the wrong enemy. First, we need a reconnaissance mission to understand the present culture of our nation. This requires discernment and relationship with those who are in the world. Then we can devise strategies to be salt and light in the real-world arena. We know that the darkness has not understood the light, but we err when the light does not understand the darkness.

---

141   Schaeffer, Francis. *A Christian Manifesto*, Crossway: Wheaton, 1981

19

America's Nemesis

———◆◆◆◆———

At what point shall we expect the approach of danger? By what means shall we fortify against it? Shall we expect some transatlantic military giant, to step the Ocean, and crush us at a blow? Never! All the armies of Europe, Asia and Africa combined, with all the treasure of the earth (our own excepted) in their military chest; with a Buonaparte for a commander, could not by force, take a drink from the Ohio, or make a track on the Blue Ridge, in a trial of a thousand years.

At what point then is the approach of danger to be expected? I answer, if it ever reach us, it must spring up amongst us. It cannot come from abroad. If destruction be our lot, we must ourselves be its author and finisher. As a nation of freemen, we must live through all time, or die by suicide.[142]

Abraham Lincoln spoke these words to a nation whose revolutionary generation had left the realm of living history to forever become history retold rather than history remembered. The experiences were now lost with those who had passed away leaving a responsibility to the generations that follow to learn from what they hoped to never need to experience. The greatest threat to America, Lincoln so eloquently proclaimed, would be internal not external. Our

---

142   Lincoln, Abraham. The Perpetuation of Our Political Institutions: Address Before the Young Men's Lyceum of Springfield, Illinois, January 27, 1838

nemesis is ourselves, more so than our foreign adversaries. In so doing, Lincoln placed the responsibility of America's destruction—should it ever be—on Americans, both as its harbinger and its finisher.

In contrast, it is a common conservative practice to blame foreign infiltrators and the previous Administration almost exclusively for the weakening of America, but this did not happen in one or two Presidential terms. America has slowly slipped from her biblical moorings. We have lost the cohesive values that enabled citizens to be as responsible as those who serve in public office for the state of our nation. The enemy of America is America.

The way forward is to stop pointing fingers and start restoring our nation brick by brick. If we do not take responsibility, who will? If Islam is our undoing, it is because we were already undone by our own corruption. If America is shaking, it is because we have forsaken our solid foundation and have built upon the sand. The bastion of Christianity retreated behind the walls of the church giving way to the secular public square. Secularism created a weakened infrastructure unable to curtail new pillars from a foreign belief system. Secularism is a homegrown philosophy, a Christian heresy. It is a Western phenomenon as it is the remnants of a former Christian culture. In a sense, it is Christianity's illegitimate offspring and thus our responsibility.

For as long as we utilize eschatology as a junk drawer for that which we do not wish to be responsible to steward, we cannot see the path that restores a nation. Anytime we place the problem out of our control, or the solution beyond our reach, our only recourse is to prepare for the inevitable or await a sovereign move of God. We left the job of building a nation to the secular world. Then we respond in anger to the state of our union, laying the blame upon them. But it is we, the believers of this nation, who have abdicated our responsibility to steward the kingdom in a manner in which builds our nation.

We may have lost ground in the process, but we cannot lose hope. We have been given a kingdom that cannot be shaken. Reforming America begins with discipling America in biblical truth. Let us not confuse discipling America with creating a theocracy or a Christian government. If we are not careful with our rhetoric, we will create fear in the populace that Christians mean to subvert the government and reinstitute a state church. The founding generation established a Republic. Reforming America restores the Republic.

Discipling America is a matter of rebuilding families, stabilizing businesses, and revitalizing our churches to standards of high integrity and civic responsibility. It is about Christians being known by our love, rather than by what we stand against. It is a matter of working in the arts and entertainment. It is a matter of restoring health care and education to their God given mandates. Removing the corruption of Washington requires discipling leaders of great character who can serve this nation without concern for job security.

We have forgotten that our battle is not against flesh and blood. We war with people instead of the spiritual atmospheric conditions that control those people. Or we solely battle in prayer and have removed ourselves from practical civic responsibility. We get involved in skirmishes and never win the war. Better yet, we fail to live from the place of the war being won. We fight from the place of the victim instead of living in the peace of victory.

Whatever we build that is not built in the peace of the kingdom will be shaken. We cannot fight out of reaction to the enemy. If we want to be an anchor in the storm, we have to stop shaking like those who have no hope. The path to standing up for America is that of laying down our lives for neighbors, co-workers, and those God gives to us to serve. It is time to replace rhetoric with practical love.

When we are shaking, we think the unshaken are either ignorant or apathetic to the problems of America. There are those who are oblivious or complacent, but others are sleeping in the boat awaiting the appointed moment to release their peace and calm a storm. Still others are working steadily from a place of peace.

Lincoln advocated that maintaining American liberty is a matter of renewing the spirit of '76—that revolutionary spirit that prevailed through the war to the establishment of the Republic. The difference is that the foundation of freedom has already been laid by those patriots of 1776. As Lincoln feared, time has eroded their memory from the world. Their spirit of patriotism lay dormant, but it is not dead. Modern debris has corrupted their memory and life's work. It is our job to dig through the debris and find the sinews of our founding history. Pulling them free from the tomb of time to reeducate a people in the ways of liberty. Then we can follow Lincoln's advice:

> [L]et every American pledge his life, his property, and his sacred honor . . . Let reverence for the laws, be breathed by every American mother, to the lisping babe, that prattles on her lap--let it be taught in schools, in seminaries, and in colleges; let it be written in Primers, spelling books, and in Almanacs;--let it be preached from the pulpit, proclaimed in legislative halls, and enforced in courts of justice. And, in short, let it become the political religion of the nation; and let the old and the young, the rich and the poor, the grave and the [joyful], of all sexes and tongues, and colors and conditions, sacrifice unceasingly upon its altars.[143]

Freedom cannot be taken for granted, that it will continue apart from studying the philosophy of freedom Lincoln calls the "political religion of the nation." Freedom requires work to sustain it. It is not entombed in the ink and parchment of the Constitution. It happens when

---

143 Ibid.

truth is cultivated in the hearts and minds of the people. A Constitutional Republic requires the Constitution and the public to sustain its vitality.

When such a sacrificial commitment is established for freedom, greater is the sustainability of that freedom. Or as Lincoln declared, "While ever a state of feeling, such as this, shall universally, or even, very generally prevail throughout the nation, vain will be every effort, and fruitless every attempt, to subvert our national freedom."[144]

---

144 Ibid.

20

Preparing to Occupy the Land

———◆◆◆———

"A Christian worldview impacts every area of life. Including making your house a home."

~ Eric Metaxas

In the first five books of the Bible, we read the history of God taking an enslaved people and making them into a great nation. A nation is more than a people group: it is a people living in their own land with their own language, government, and law. A great nation is a people who do this within the biblical context of what it means to be a nation that blesses other nations.

While camped at Mount Sinai, God begins to provide the instructions that will enable them to become a great nation. God teaches them law, sanitation, justice, social responsibility, agriculture, etc. In the middle of all this instruction, God tells His people that He is not going to drive out all those who occupy the land for them until they are ready to possess it.

Consider what God says:

"But I will not drive them out in a single year, because the land would become desolate and wild animals too

numerous for you. Little by little I will drive them out before you, until you have increased enough to take possession of the land. I will establish your borders from the Red Sea to the Mediterranean Sea, and from the desert to the Euphrates River. I will give into your hands the people who lived in the land, you will drive them out before you" (Exodus 23:29-31, NIV).

God did not want the land to lay desolate and become wild and untamed, so He allowed people who were not His people to occupy the land.

When a place is cleared out of its occupants before it is able to be filled with God's purpose, it becomes a magnet for a greater darkness than its previous occupants.

We read of this in the New Testament.

"When an impure spirit comes out of a person, it goes through arid places seeking rest and does not find it. Then it says, 'I will return to the house I left.' When it arrives, it finds the house unoccupied, swept clean and put in order. Then it goes and takes with it seven other spirits more wicked than itself, and they go in and live there. And the final condition of that person is worse than the first. That is how it will be with this wicked generation" (Matthew 12:42-45 NIV).

Even though this passage is talking about evil spirits, the principle works with regards to removing those who occupy without properly replacing that occupier. We see this when a dictator is removed without the ability to replace him with a healthier form of government. Typically, this causes the present government to topple and a greater evil to fill its place.

Consider this in the context of America. If an industry is occupied by the world, and we seek to remove those occupiers before we are ready to fill the void, something more powerful will fill it for us. Instead of trying to unseat the powers that exist, we may want to consider training believers to begin to shine in those places of influence until they become the leaders themselves. Otherwise, we push out those who are keeping the industry, mountain, or sphere in society from desolation.

Biased journalism is better than no journalism. Journalism is the eyes and ears of a free nation. It operates as a check and balance on the government. Even a corrupt media reporting through biased lenses gets vital information out to the public. If we are not careful, we will cost our nation the power of the pen instead of reforming the institution unto its purpose.

Mediocre secularized public education is better than no national education. One of the key principles of a free people is the education of the common people, not just the elite. An educated people are a check on government. We cannot remove what we have without something better to replace it with.

Perhaps we can gain a more appreciative outlook on those who are occupying what we are not occupying yet. Maybe we can see them as playing a part in the sustaining of our national spheres of influence rather than the destroyers of our nation. We may have developed Christian news sites and Christian education, but we no longer occupy the national system. Until we do, we need these systems in place in our nation even though they are influenced by a secular worldview. If we want to reform the nation, we may want to consider working to reform the existing spheres of influence by going into the high places of culture with the kingdom of God.

The world is good at discipling. The secular worldview is promoted unashamedly in every sphere of society. It has permeated culture. We often think that people know better than to teach a view that is not biblical. This leads us to think that those who occupy the high places of culture intentionally want to cause harm because we know their worldview is harmful. But people cannot see their own error.

Most cultural influences are not trying to lead people away from truth—they are simply convinced of their own way of thinking and live it out in the real world. They may have agendas that are antithetical to Christianity, but their agendas are in line with their thinking and they believe them to be good and noble. They do not know different. These influencers are not our enemy—our enemy has deceived them. Even still they play a vital role in keeping out greater darkness while we learn to become the influencers God has called us to be in our nation.

Reforming America means we become reformers of America. Reformation is about influencing a nation in all the areas that makes it a great nation. The Hebrew people did not know how to be a nation. They had to be taught everything: what to do with waste, disease, how to grow crops and raise livestock, how to deal with conflict, how to raise children, how to worship God, how to create a legal system and a government, and so much more.

The Bible is not just instruction for our spirituality, but practical instruction for our way of life as a nation. This is the job of the church—the body of believers working as we once worked when the Bible birthed the West.

21

The Bible Makes Great Nations

———◆◆◆◆◆———

*"In the beginning, America was Protestant: that point has been
emphasized by every historian of the United States."*

~ Russell Kirk

History affirms the power of the Bible to transform
nations. In 2017 we celebrated the 500th anniversary of the
Protestant Reformation. Many of the nations of the world
enjoy the fruit of applied biblical theology. We enjoy this
fruit because Martin Luther, John Calvin, John Huss, and
John Wycliff laid down their lives to live out the truth of
the Bible. Many more names belong in this list of honored
reformers and Bible translators, but the reason we can name
any is because they made the Bible the standard throughout
the world.

If you call Barnes & Noble and ask what the number one
bestselling book is, they will tell you: The Bible. We still buy it
in record numbers, but do we still reform our nation with it?

The reason America was a Christian nation is because
of our Bible-based foundational worldview. The reason
America is now considered post-Christian is because we are
rapidly losing that worldview. Christian thinker and author,
Os Guinness, opines in his book *Impossible People* that

"while the West is no longer Christian . . . it is not yet fully non-Christian (secularist or pagan) either . . . it is in a post-Christian phase."[145]

The good news is that the Gospel is still Good News. It has the same reforming power it has always contained. It has not changed. Its truth still liberates. Its truth still transforms. To quote Os Guinness once more, "Doom, gloom, alarmism and fear are never the way for the people of God."[146]

What has changed is our belief in the Bible. Our belief has changed enough that America is rightly classified as post-Christian. In fact, the *Oxford English Dictionary* named the 2016 word of the year as "post-truth."

In contrast, "in the world of the Founders, the Bible was an unavoidable and useful rod of measurement, a stimulus to intellectual innovation."[147] The famed conservative writer, Russell Kirk states in his book *The Roots of American Order* that: "In the beginning, America was Protestant: that point has been emphasized by every historian of the United States."[148] America is the fruit of the Reformation's applied biblical theology.

Francis Schaffer wrote:

The Reformation with its emphasis upon the Bible, in all that it teaches, as being the revelation of God, provided a freedom in society and yet a form in society as well. Thus, there were freedoms in the Reformation countries (such as the world had never known before) without these freedoms leading to chaos—because both laws and morals

---

145 Guinness, Os, *Impossible People: Christian Courage and the Struggle for the Soul of Civilization* (Downers Grove: IVP Books, 2016) p. 39

146 Ibid, p. 33

147 Novak, Michael, *On Two Wings: Humble Faith and Common Sense at the America's Founding* (New York: Encounter Books, 2002) p. 28

148 Kirk, Russell, *The Roots of American Order* (Wilmington: Intercollegiate Studies Institute, 2002) p. 229

were surrounded by a consensus resting upon what the Bible taught. . .[149]

History is replete with evidence of the power of the Bible to create great nations. We do not find free nations without the Bible at their core. Anywhere we find truth liberating the people, we find the Bible behind it. We see this in the life of William Wilberforce, John Wesley, and William Carey. We see throughout history from Martin Luther to Martin Luther King, Jr. Our Founders understood the indispensable necessity for the Bible to undergird all we do as a nation.

Benjamin Rush, signer of the Declaration of Independence, Surgeon General of the Continental Army, and father of the United States Public Schools, wrote:

[T]he Bible… should be read in our schools in preference to all other books because it contains the greatest portion of that kind of knowledge which is calculated to produce private and public happiness.[150]

Noah Webster wrote in the same vein:

[O]ur citizens should early understand that the genuine source of correct republican principles is the Bible, particularly the New Testament, or the Christian religion. [T]he Christian religion is the most important and one of the first things in which all children under a free government ought to be instructed. No truth is more evident than that the Christian religion must be the basis of any government intended to secure the rights and privileges of a free people.[151]

---

149 Schaeffer, Francis, *The Great Evangelical Disaster* (Wheaton: Crossway Books, 1984) p. 47

150 Benjamin Rush, *Essays, Literary, Moral & Philosophical* (Philadelphia: Thomas & Samuel F. Bradford, 1798), pp. 94, 100, "A Defence of the Use of the Bible as a School Book."

151 Noah Webster, *A Collection of Papers on Political, Literary, and Moral Subjects* (New York: Webster and Clark, 1843), p. 291, from his "Reply to a Letter of David McClure on the Subject of the Proper Course of Study in the Girard College, Philadelphia. New Haven, October 25, 1836." Noah Webster, *History of the United States* (New Haven: Durrie and Peck, 1832), p. 6.

We are at a juncture in American history where reinstituting the Bible into our way of life as a nation will not only be a reformation, but a revolution. The only way we can pull our Christian heritage into tomorrow is to start afresh today. Instead of lamenting what was, becoming depressed about what is, or afraid of what will be, we can start where we are today.

The Bible reforms as well today as it did in pagan Rome. The Bible reforms today as well as it did in Victorian England when the first evangelicals became serious about living out the Bible.[152] The Bible reforms today as well as it did when William Carey took it to India where the fruit of his work lives on.[153] And it reforms today as well as it has for five hundred years since Martin Luther nailed his 95 Theses on the door of the Wittenberg church.

We do not want the Bible to become so commonplace on our bookshelves that it is not commonplace in our lives. The first step to reformation is a Bible believing and practicing church. We live in a free nation because Martin Luther read the Bible and believed it. He practiced its truth to the extent that his life was constantly in danger.

Today, we fight culture to allow us our freedom to publicly express our faith. But what if we fought with that same tenacity to live out the Bible in our homes, workplaces, and churches? I am not speaking of a war against culture, but of transforming it because we overcame our own failure to conform to Scripture. When our lives glow with the fruit of living out the Bible, the world will notice.

China is looking for a worldview to replace Marxism. They want something that will sustain their nation. They are

---

152 Bradley, Ian. *The Call to Seriousness: The Evangelical Impact on the Victorians*, Lion Books; London, November 17, 2006.

153 Mangalwadi, Vishal and Ruth, *The Legacy of William Carey: A Model for the Transformation of Culture* (Wheaton: Crossway Books, 1999)

seriously considering Christianity, but they do not understand why we are walking away from it. They wonder why the West is moving away from what they see as giving it its success.[154]

My question is: how does our generation see the success of the Bible lived out unless we live it? We cannot start with it in our public schools until we start with it in our homes. When the world sees the transformational power of living biblical lives, they will want what we have. History proves this maxim. Let us make history by making the Bible our standard once again.

154 Guinness, Os, *Impossible People: Christian Courage and the Struggle for the Soul of Civilization* (Downers Grove: IVP Books, 2016), Chapter 1

22

Preserving Biblical Revelation

"The Bible is not merely a handbook of private piety. It is the very foundation of Western Civilization."

- Vishal Mangalwadi

We cannot have truth without revelation. Without revelation all claims to truth are equally valid or invalid human inventions. Who can claim one idea as superior to another because all are equally human? Who is to say one human's thoughts about the world are any better than the next person's?

However, God did not leave us in confusion. He provided us with revelation that is found in one book, the Bible. The Bible is real truth. It is "true truth," to borrow from Francis Schaeffer. Its author is God and its writers are people who wrote down what the Lord inspired them to write. It is true history. It is true science. It is true testimony. God really said what it says He said. He really did what it says He did. He really will do what it says He will do.

We have history and science today because the Bible gives us the foundation for these disciplines to grow in stable ground. The idea that we can measure, catalog, and classify the natural world is a creation of the Bible's impact on our thinking. If we do not know our history, we will make the grave mistake in thinking that we have always thought this way. When we think our thinking is common sense, we will not work to preserve this special knowledge in our culture.

The Bible is not Jesus. Jesus is the Truth. It is because Truth is a person that truth can be found in the pages of a book about the Person of Truth. The Holy Spirit leads us into all truth, but He will never lead us in something that contradicts what the Bible truly teaches.

What I have written above is a timeless hallmark of Christian thinking. In our post-Christian world, ideas are emerging about the Bible that are derived from outside influences. If Paul was writing, he would say "who has bewitched us"?

One of these influences is atheism, specifically the writings of Richard Dawkins, Christopher Hitchens, and Sam Harris. These atheists champion the idea that the Christian God depicted in the Old Testament is an abominable monster of a God. These writers borrow from the biblical worldview to judge the God of the Bible. They not only judge Him, but singlehandedly convict Him of their charges. Leaving aside the myriad of responses one can give to atheism, we move on to look at what this philosophy is now doing inside Christianity.

Philosophies outside of the church seldom stay outside. Francis Schaeffer once wrote, "Tell me what the world is saying today, and I'll tell you what the church will be saying in seven years." Sadly, atheistic biblical interpretation is starting to seep into the church. Some Christians now look at the Old Testament and see a horrific story (not history) that, if true, makes God out to be a monster. These believers cannot reconcile Jesus of the New Testament with God's recorded actions of the Old Testament. The solution has become to consider the Old Testament as myth and not history, at least in the parts that supposedly gives God a bad name. This is not good theology. This is evidence of Christians being discipled by atheists without knowing the source of their new-found worldview.

All ideas come from somewhere. When "new" ideas come to biblical interpretation they either come from the Bible or they come from another influence and invade biblical interpretation in a manner that kills truth.

I remember sitting in my college literature class learning literary criticism theories. One student turned to me and said, "If this is how to interpret literature, then we have to apply this to the Bible too." I firmly and swiftly asserted that the literary theory we were being taught was not a good way to interpret the Bible. She disagreed.

We are learning to think like those who bring outside accusations to the text and thus to God that are not part of our tradition. When we think like this, we are seeing the Bible like atheists instead of like Christians. Yet we have a real relationship with Jesus, and we know how to hear the Holy Spirit. We know God to be real and active in our lives. Since we know Jesus to be real, we think we have to come up with new biblical interpretations to explain away these so-called embarrassing passages that we now see through our cultural conditioning.

However, the Bible is counterculture. We do not bring our meaning to the text; we get our truth from the text. Our culture cannot come to bear on Scripture; Scripture must come to bear on our culture.

One of the difficulties is taking a tolerance influenced secularized interpretation of the word "good" and judging God's works based on that postmodern concept. We do not dispense with the understanding that God is good. But if the words of the Bible disagree with our concept of "goodness" we find an interpretation that validates our meaning of the word. In so doing, we interpret the Bible based on our culture instead of getting at the real meaning of the text.

This is postmodernism. This is French literary philosophy applied to the Bible. Jacques Derrida (the French philosopher famous for birthing postmodern philosophy) teaches that the author is dead. We bring our own meaning to any book, art, or music, and we determine what it means for us. There is no author to give it meaning, for the author does not have a right to infuse it with meaning for the reader. The reader partakes of it from whatever perspective the reader wants to impose upon it. Instead of retaining the integrity of the text and learning what the author is saying, we seek what we receive from our reading of it combined with what we bring to it. It is believed it is impossible to do otherwise.

In postmodern biblical interpretation, we are not seeking understanding from the text. Instead, we come to it as a corrupted document full of cultural influences taking it away from the purity of God's inspiration. We approach it as a human work with dead authors that we now get to wrestle with in our day and our interpretation believing that no one can ever get at its integral meaning. To do this is to not only be discipled by atheism, but by postmodernism.

It is ironic in a postmodern age that we are interpreting the Bible to be written by postmodern storytellers instead of servants of a living God who wrote down His sacred revelation. We err when we use the philosophy of the day to create a revolution in biblical interpretation. Martin Luther led a Reformation because he read the Bible and believed what God said, and now we want to believe modern authors who tell us that mere men wrote the Bible and God did not really say and did not really do what the Bible says He said and did.

We serve a living God. The Author of the Bible is very much alive. The meaning He infused in the Bible has not changed from the day it was first penned on papyrus scrolls. Our job is to get at that meaning and to have it inform our theology. We will not get at that meaning perfectly. We will see in part and not see what we see clearly because we are human. We do, in fact, have cultural influences crowding in on our thinking. But the truth does not change. It is we who change to conform to the truth as we grow in understanding of Scripture and as we grow up into Christ.

The existence of an absolute true God and His absolutely true ways does not give us license to be absolutely certain we absolutely know all God has said and meant perfectly. It means there is truth outside of ourselves. Our interpretations and our thinking are measured against it. The goal is to grow in the truth. We do not size up the Bible, it sizes us up.

If our worldview shifts away from the veracity of the Bible to philosophy that undermines its integrity, we move farther away from that which will transform nations. Only when we see the Bible as true revelation, like Martin Luther did, will we see our nation and the nations of this world restored to their intended purpose and glory.

"Your word is a lamp to my feet
And a light to my path.

I have sworn and I will confirm it,
That I will keep Your righteous ordinances.

I am exceedingly afflicted;
Revive me, O Lord, according to Your word.

O accept the freewill offerings of my mouth, O Lord,
And teach me Your ordinances.

My life is continually in my hand,
Yet I do not forget Your law.

The wicked have laid a snare for me,
Yet I have not gone astray from Your precepts.
I have inherited Your testimonies forever,
For they are the joy of my heart.

I have inclined my heart to perform Your
statutes Forever, *even* to the end" (Psalm
119:105-112).

23

Bridging the Gap Between Secular and Sacred

<hr>

"We are all priests before God, there is no such distinction as 'secular or sacred.' In fact, the opposite of sacred is not secular; the opposite of sacred is profane. In short, no follower of Christ does secular work. We all have a sacred calling."

~ Ravi Zacharias

Discipling nations in truth will not be accomplished in one generation. It is something that must be passed on from one generation to the next. It will also take a concerted effort across denominational and ethnic lines to provide the cohesive holistic discipleship our nation so desperately needs.

But one person, or small team of people, can make a huge difference. We still know the names of Noah Webster, William McGuffey, William Wilberforce, Hannah More, Martin Luther, John Calvin, William Carey, George Washington, Adam Smith, John Locke, George Washington Carver, and Martin Luther King, Jr. because of their contributions to public truth. We believe slavery is wrong because William Wilberforce worked tirelessly to bring that biblical truth to bear upon society. It took time for that truth to work its way down to abolish slavery altogether, but there is no doubt that it is a biblical worldview that undergirds the right to human dignity and equality. Martin Luther King, Jr. gave his life to the eradication of racism and inequality in this nation. When a person steps out to reform a nation to truth, we never forget his or her name.

The great impediment to reforming nations is the worldview that divides what is sacred from what is secular. Only a false worldview creates a dichotomy between secular and sacred when there ought not to be any division. This worldview is held both by Christians and secularists alike. The mythic belief that there is public and private truth, or secular and religious truth, has affected us all. The concept goes back to Plato but has taken many forms.

Plato opined that the real substance of a thing existed in an other-worldly state he called "Forms." He argued that what we see on the earth is a shadow copy of the real and not the true state of a thing.[155] The tree we see in our yard is not the real tree. The real tree is in another place where the real form of the tree exists. The church before the Reformation adopted this idea in a semi-Christianized application that the real purpose of man is found in spiritual pursuits and not in the real life of everyday living. Thus, the cloistered life of monasteries became superior to the life of the non-monastic society. Martin Luther rejected this dichotomy and we see biblical theology exploding through the Protestant Reformation into all the spheres of society: marriage, business, economics, arts, music, education, etc. Cities and nations began to flourish in a new way because Protestant theology did not divide secular and sacred.

What it did do, in time, was divide the institution of the state from the institution of the church. The biblical idea of freedom of religion required this separation. However, it

---

155 Pearcey, Nancy. *Total Truth: Liberating Christianity From Its Cultural Captivity.* (Wheaton: Crossway Books, 2008) p. 74-75

did not separate God's truth from government. Separation of church and state was never intended to be separation of God and state. It is biblical truth that provides the theology to keep these two institutions separate, but to forsake that biblical truth is to endanger religious freedom.

The Reformation repaired the breach of secular and sacred, but we live in a world that has lost that truth. In the church, we elevate the spiritual life and Christian callings to ministerial work over the marketplace and "secular life." Our discipleship is designed around how to live like Jesus morally and spiritually, but (in most cases) not how to develop one's profession along the lines of biblical theology. Discipleship once entailed botany, gardening, farming, cooking, hygiene, and all kinds of equipping for daily life.

In the world, the emphasis is placed on the "secular and public side" of life. The institutions of culture run like a machine, yet they are severed from their biblical origins. They cannot run long term without the worldview engine to fuel and direct their progress. The world considers the worldview element to be "private truth." The postmodern world does not deem "private truth" truth at all, for it has now been downgraded to the story one believes about life. However, there is no such thing as a neutral worldview. Secularism, postmodernism, and atheism each have their own way of looking at the world. It is a myth that we can or should keep our theology, philosophy, and worldview as private truth that does not affect the public world.

Christians have bought into this myth. When we strive for a place in the marketplace, we often do so looking to wear a cross, sport a Christian tee-shirt, have a lunch time prayer meeting, or host a Bible study at work. Perhaps we openly evangelize our co-workers and customers, but that is usually as far as it goes. The Bible is not just for our spiritual lives and the saving of our souls—it's for the entire way in which life is done in a nation. Its truth applies to every institution and academic discipline. A Christian company is not one with a fish in its logo; it is one that has applied biblical truth to how it operates and how it develops its industry. It is not about how many Christians the company employs, but how Christian the company's theology and practice of work is. To do this will require an entire paradigm shift in how we approach our industry.

How does the Bible shape business, economics, government, sports, arts, law, farming, the health care industry, hospice, science, births, deaths, marriage, counseling, anthropology? Most of the way in which we approach the myriad of disciplines and spheres of society still carry the Christian worldview, or else these institutions would have long since completed their decay. If we do not pick up where we left off in discipling institutions in God's truth, we will continue to witness chronic decay.

Faith can be a personal matter, but truth is always public. When we privatize Christianity, we are not just keeping our moral opinions and spiritual beliefs at home, we are keeping truth siloed from the rest of the world. We owe the world truth.

Nancy Pearcey writes, "We have to insist on presenting Christianity as a comprehensive unified worldview that addresses all of life and reality. It is not just religious truth but total truth."[156] We cannot see America reformed any other way. The biblical worldview has no cultural divide between private truth and public truth. The only division should be between truth and lies. We cannot build a nation on lies or faulty worldviews. We live in a nation built on truth. It is our responsibility to reform it according to that biblical truth. We

---

156 Pearcey, p. 111

do not do it through force, fear, manipulation, or power, but through love married to truth. When we lay our lives down for the good of our nation—sacrificing our prestige, notoriety, and the right to be right for the privilege to serve and show a better way forward—we will see a nation reformed.

Appendix:

Reforming Marriage

"Real love, the Bible says, instinctively desires permanence."

- Timothy Keller

We live in a world where it takes two to get married and only one to get divorced. Marriage requires two willing people to join in holy matrimony, whereas divorce needs only one person to legally walk away, even if there are no grounds to do so. Such is the world of the no-fault divorce.

About fifty years ago Ronald Reagan, then governor of California, signed into law a bill that granted no-fault divorces in the State of California. Over the next decade, the states followed suit leaving New York as the only state without no-fault divorce.

Prior to a no-fault divorce, the law required a criminal reason for the divorce. Adultery, cruelty, and desertion were criminal behaviors. Thus, one person filed a Complaint of Divorce and the other party became the defendant. With no-fault divorces, one party, who has not done anything criminal to the other party, can be made the defendant simply because one or both parties do not wish to continue to be married. Sadly, there is no legal recourse for the party who does not want a divorce. The law does not protect such a one.

Moreover, the one committing the crime was not the one filing for divorce. The Complaint was issued against the one who had harmed the marriage through desertion, cruelty, or adultery. The offender became the defendant as one would in criminal court. The Complainant would have to prove that the alleged grounds against the Defendant were true for the divorce to be granted. Divorce then was treated as the serious matter that it is, not as something one could casually acquire.

We often move the conversation into how it takes two people to make a marriage work, thereby arguing that it takes two to make it fail. In the popular way we look at marriage today this is true, but there was a day before irreconcilable differences became a way to describe a failed marriage. Marriage is not supposed to be easy. Martin Luther called marriage "a school of character." It did more to make him Christ-like than monastic life ever could.

When we do not get along, it is not evidence of marital problems, but of character problems starting with our own. The marriage is not the problem, our own hearts are the problem. The solution is love. We only get in trouble when we stop loving. Let's consider it all joy every time we have a new opportunity to learn forgiveness, patience, and self-control. In this way, we cannot point blame, but only take responsibility. It's not "I shouldn't have to forgive you," it's "I get to forgive you." It is a great opportunity to practice love at higher and higher levels.

Sometimes we have neglected our relationship for a long time. It is like when you leave your lawn unattended. The grass and weeds can grow up to your waste. Thistles and thorns wend their way across the front walk. However, the solution is not moving to a new house; it's beginning to tend what you had previously neglected. You work on it a little at a time giving it the nurture and nutrients it needs to be a well-manicured lawn. In the same way, if you begin to tend your neglected marriage, it will grow healthy again.

I have worked as a paralegal for almost two decades. One day a lady asked me if I would use my boss's services for my divorce. I opened my mouth and shut it again. I pondered how to answer such a question. A photograph from my wedding sits on my desk depicting a happy bride and groom. Finally, I spoke. "I know what you're asking, but I can't answer your question that way because I will not be getting divorced." Before I could say more, she reacted, "You don't know that." I assured her I did, but she wasn't convinced. Instead of trying to convince her, I simply affirmed that my boss is good at his job.

I've lived a lot more life since that day. I still hold to what I said, though I have witnessed far too many broken marriages. No marriage is invincible. Each one takes an abundance of love and forgiveness. But we do not move the standard when the standard is not kept or achieved. We cannot change God's ways when our ways fall short. Forgiveness would lose its power if the standard moved every time we failed to live up to it. There is no condemnation for those who are in Christ Jesus, but there is a standard. To be clear, the biblical standard is one man married in covenant to one woman before God, for life.

Because of sin, lots of other marriage situations exist, but it does not make any of them the standard. God will not love you less because your marriage failed, and because He won't love you less, He won't reduce His standard. Jesus forgave the woman caught in adultery and told her to go and sin no more. We can only start from where we are at to begin to do things God's way.

Marriage is a safeguard for the family, especially for women and children. Vishal Mangalwadi explains that, "When a husband is forbidden extramarital affairs, taking a second wife, or divorcing a difficult wife; when he is not allowed to hate or be harsh with her; when he is required to love and honor his wife; then his wife is empowered."[157] Our state laws used to protect marriage thereby protecting the family and the stability of our nation. The more we digress from a biblical moral code, the more our laws fail to reflect God's ways.

The world's laws do not set the way for us as Christians. Marriage and divorce laws change with culture, but not with God. Biblical truth created the modern world because it did not conform to the world. The more the modern world stops conforming to truth, the less modern it will be. We are entering a post-modern world, a world that is characterized by being "post-truth." The world before biblical truth civilized it, was a pre-modern, pagan world. The more post-truth we become, the more paganism we will return to as a society.

The breakdown of marriage in a society is as detrimental as, or maybe even more so than, government corruption. It destroys the society from within, breaking down its families and moral character. The Lord is not looking for guilt, but for repentance. He wants us to change the way we think, to come up to a higher way of living, rather than settling for broken standards and worldly ways of living. Many societies, more corrupt than our own, have restored marriage and the family to society. We do not have to wait for laws to change for hearts to change. Reforming the way the world does marriage starts with reforming the way we do marriage. Reformation begins with the church.

Works Cited

Adams, John (President) to the Officers of the First Brigade of the Third Division of the Militia of Massachusetts, 1798 http://johnadamscenter.com/who-we-are/why-john-adams/

Amos, Gary T. *Defending the Declaration*. Wolgemuth & Hyatt: Brentwood, 1989

Barton, David "John Locke: Deist or Theologian" http://www.wallbuilders.com/libissuesarticles.asp?id=106

Benjamin Rush, *Essays, Literary, Moral & Philosophical* (Philadelphia: Thomas & Samuel F. Bradford, 1798), pp. 94, 100, "A Defence of the Use of the Bible as a School Book."

Bradley, Ian. *The Call to Seriousness: The Evangelical Impact on the Victorians*, Lion Books; London, November 17, 2006.

Cadei, Emily, *Newsweek: How Corporate America Propelled Same-Sex Marriage*. June 30, 2015. http://www.newsweek.com/2015/07/10/shift-corporate-america-social-issues-become-good-business-348458.html

Chesterton, G.K. *What's Wrong with the World*. Dover: New York, 1910 & 2007

Ellis, Joseph. *The Quartet: Orchestrating the Second American Revolution*, 1783-1789 (New York; Penguin Random House, LLC, 2015

Federer, William J. *America's God and Country* (America: Fame Publishing, Inc. 1996) p. 637.

George Mason Bio. http://www.gunstonhall.org/georgemason/

Guinness, Os, *Impossible People: Christian Courage and the Struggle for the Soul of Civilization* (Downers Grove: IVP Books, 2016)

Higginbotham, Don. *George Washington Uniting a Nation* (Oxford: Rowan Littlefield Publishers, Inc., 2002) p. 53.

The History Place http://www.historyplace.com/speeches/washington.htm

Hoffding, Herald. *A History of Modern Philosophy: A Sketch of the History of Philosophy.* Andover: Cambridge, 1900

Kuyper, Abraham. *Lectures on Calvinism.*, USA:ReadaClassic. com, 2010

Kirk, Russell, *The Roots of American Order* (Wilmington: Intercollegiate Studies Institute, 2002)

Lewis, C.S. *Miracles.*

Locke, John. *Second Treatise of Government.* Barnes and Noble: New York, 1690 and 2004,

Locke, John. *A Letter Concerning Toleration.* 1689. http://presspubs. uchicago.edu/founders/documents/amendI_religions10.html

Lodge, Henry Cabot. *George Washington. Vol II*, (Boston: Houghton, Mifflin & Co. 1898) p. 29.

Madison, James. *The Federalist Papers*, Penguin Books: New York

Mangalwadi, Vishal. *The Book the Made Your World.* Nashville, Thomas Nelson, 2011

Mangalwadi, Vishal and Ruth, *The Legacy of William Carey: A Model for the Transformation of Culture* (Wheaton: Crossway Books, 1999)

Mangalwadi, Vishal BLUE: *Mother Earth Should Take Care of Us.* Video by Vishal Mangalwadi. https://www.youtube.com/ watch?v=8XeO0MQqimc

Marsden, George. *The Soul of the American University from Protestant Establishment to Established Nonbelief.* Oxford: Oxford University Press, 1994.

McGuffey, William H., *McGuffey's New Eclectic Third Reader.* Ohio: Hinkle and Wilson, 1865.

Novak, Michael, *On Two Wings: Humble Faith and Common Sense at the America's Founding* (New York: Encounter Books, 2002)

Pearcey, Nancy. *Total Truth: Liberating Christianity From Its Cultural Captivity.* (Wheaton: Crossway Books, 2008)

Phelps, Glenn. *George Washington and American Constitutionalism* (Kansas: University Press of Kansas: 1993) p. 126-133.

Rozell, Mark J. ed. *George Washington and the Origins of the American Presidency* (Connecticut: Praeger Publishers, 2000) p. 95.

Schaeffer, Francis. *A Christian Manifesto*, Crossway: Wheaton, 1981

Schaeffer, Francis, *The Great Evangelical Disaster* (Wheaton: Crossway Books, 1984)

Smith, Roy C. *Adam Smith and the Origins of American Enterprise*, Truman Talley Books. New York, 2004

Smith, Adam. *The Wealth of Nations*. Barnes & Noble. New York, 2004 (1776)

Stark, Rodney. *Victory of Reason*. New York; Random House, 2005

Stark, Rodney. *For the Glory of God*. Princeton University Press; New Jersey, 2003

The George Washington Papers: http://gwpapers.virginia.edu/exhibits/mourning/response.html

Washington, George. *The Writings of Washington, Vol. X* (Boston: Hilliard, Gray & Co., 1836.) p. 69-72.

Weathersby, Danielle & Day, Terri, *Fortune: How Walmart Could Get Congress to Reform America's Gun Control Laws*. June 25, 2015 http://fortune.com/2015/06/25/how-walmart-could-get-congress-to-reform-americas-gun-control-laws/

Webster, Noah, *A Collection of Papers on Political, Literary, and Moral Subjects* (New York: Webster and Clark, 1843), p. 291, from his "Reply to a Letter of David McClure on the Subject of the Proper Course of Study in the Girard College, Philadelphia. New Haven, October 25, 1836."

Webster Noah, *History of the United States* (New Haven: Durrie and Peck, 1832), p. 6.

Westerhoff, John H. III. *McGuffey and His Readers: Piety, Morality and Education in Nineteenth-Century America*. Milford, Motts Media, Inc. 1982

Recommended Reading

Back to the Future: Rebuilding America's Stability
By Karla Perry

If You Can Keep It: The Forgotten Promise of American Liberty
By Eric Metaxas

*The Book That Made Your World: How the Bible Created the
Soul of Western Civilization*
By Vishal Mangalwadi

*This Book Changed Everything: The Bible's Amazing Impact on
our World, Vol 1*
By Vishal Mangalwadi

Liberating the Nations
By Stephen McDowell and Mark Beliles

*Impossible People: Christian Courage and the Struggle for the
Soul of Civilization*
By Os Guinness

*A Free People's Suicide: Sustainable Freedom and The American
Future*
By Os Guinness

The Call to Seriousness: The Evangelical Impact on the Victorians
By Ian Bradley

About the Author

Karla Perry, worldview revitalizer and author of *Back to the Future: Rebuilding America's Stability*, is an avid writer with a penetrating and thought-provoking style. Karla helps people develop healthy worldviews through biblical Kingdom-based thinking. She earned her bachelor's degree from Old Dominion University where she majored in English and minored in American history. Karla is a co-founder of The Serve Initiative; a think tank and task force organization designed to equip and empower believers for the work of reformation. Karla lives with her husband, Joseph, in Virginia Beach, VA where they pastored for eleven years. You can find more of Karla's work at www.karlaperry.com

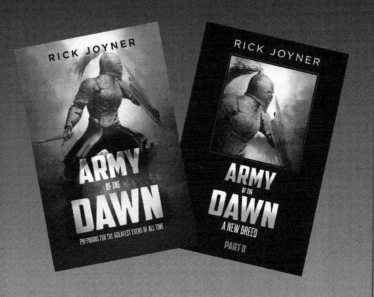

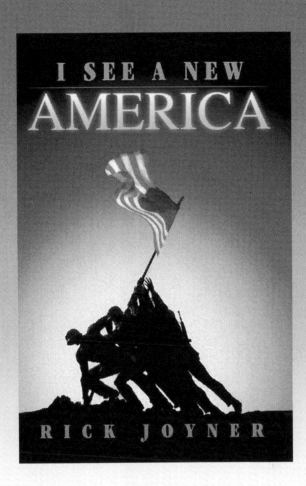

PARTNERS

Our MorningStar Partners have grown into an extraordinary global fellowship of men and women who are committed to seeing The Great Commission fulfilled in our times. Join us in equipping the body of Christ through conferences, schools, media, and publications.

We are committed to multiplying the impact of the resources entrusted to us. Your regular contribution of any amount—whether it's once a month or once a year—will make a difference!

In His Service,

PARTNER WITH US TODAY

63511735R00097

Made in the USA
Middletown, DE
26 August 2019